Alexander Radcliffe

Ovid Travestie

A Burlesque upon Ovid's Epistles

Alexander Radcliffe

Ovid Travestie
A Burlesque upon Ovid's Epistles

ISBN/EAN: 9783337205454

Printed in Europe, USA, Canada, Australia, Japan

Cover: Foto ©Thomas Meinert / pixelio.de

More available books at **www.hansebooks.com**

Two hundred and fifty copies only (all on the same paper) have been printed of this volume, and the type has been distributed.

No. 128

OVID TRAVESTIE

A

BURLESQUE

UPON

OVID'S EPISTLES

BY

Captain ALEXANDER RADCLIFFE, of

GRAYS-INN

𝔓𝔯𝔦𝔳𝔞𝔱𝔢 𝔎𝔢𝔭𝔯𝔦𝔫𝔱

M DCCC LXXXIX

*a**

The TABLE.

INTRODUCTORY NOTE.

APTAIN Alexander Radcliffe's book was originally issued in the year 1680 and met with such appreciation that a second and enlarged edition was issued in 1681, and a fourth edition in 1705. Notwithstanding this, "OVID TRAVESTIE" has always been a scarce work, and copies of it are now practically unprocurable, except at the prohibitive price of several guineas each. That it merits a place in every collector's library is undisputed, its singularly easy strain of wit, and ludicrous parody of Ovid's famed *Heroïdes*, shewing Capt. Radcliffe to possess not only an intimate knowledge of Ovid's manner, but a graphic power of turning to ridicule his author's most poetic flights.

Still, "OVID TRAVESTIE" is not a volume fitted for the ordinary bookshelf. Speech two hundred years

ago was far freer than in our present day, and it cannot be denied that Capt. Radcliffe was as great a sinner
in this respect as any of his contemporaries. Many
passages in his book are far too coarse to suit the taste
of our modern circulating-library subscribers, and
for these the present issue is not intended. It is
essentially a book for the student, the collector, and
such as can enjoy a hearty laugh without caring to
apply the strict rules which seem to govern the pro-
duction of our literature of to-day. Coarseness
apart, Capt. Radcliffe has most felicitously caught
and reproduced the turns of speech of his original,
and the lightness and genuine humour of his style
will be no less appreciated by his present readers
than they were on the original issue of the book.

The present reprint is made verbatim from the
fourth and complete edition (A.D. 1705).

TO

ROBERT FAIRBEARD

OF

GRAYS-INN, *Esquire.*

SIR,

*H*AVING *committed these Epistles to the* Press, *I
was horribly put to't for a Patron : I thought of
some great Lord, or some Angelick Lady ; but then again
consider'd I should never be able to adorn my Dedication
with benign Beams, coruscant Rays, and the Devil and all
of Influence. At last I heard my good Friend Mr.* Fair-
beard *was come to Town—nay then all's well enough. To
you therefore I offer this English* Ovid, *to whom you may
not be unaptly Compar'd in several Parcels of your Life
and Conversation ; only with this Exception, That you
have nothing of his* Tristibus *you.*

*'Tis you who Burlesque all the Foppery and conceited
Gravity of the Age. I remember you once told a grave*

I

affected Advocate, That he Burlesqu'd God's Image, for God had made him after his own Likeness, but he made himself look like an Ass.

Upon the whole Matter I am very well satisfy'd of my Choice of you for my Judge; if you speak well of the Book, 'tis all I desire, and the Bookseller will have reason to rejoice: tho' by your Approbation you may draw upon your self a grand Inconvenience; for perhaps you may too often have Songs, Sonnets, Madrigals, and an innumerable Army of Stanza's obtruded upon you by

Sir,

Octob, 28*th.*   Your humble Servant,
1680

Alex. Radicliffe.

TO THE READER.

Occasion'd by the PREFACE to a late Book call'd

THE WITS PARAPHRAS'D.

BEFORE I shall give you any **Account of our Old** Friend *Ovid*, or of his *Life*, I am to **inform** you, that his *Epistles* have been ingeniously **and correctly** translated **by** several **Gentlemen; and withal,** that he **was** of a good Family, **and a brave** Fellow was he. Now, since the unhappy **Accident** of his Death, his Ghost has been lately attempted **to** be rais'd by an unlucky *Pretender* to *Poetry*, who indeed hath not Skill enough to disturb his Manes; He calls his Book, *The Wits Paraphras'd,* or, *Paraphrase upon Paraphrase,* that is, *Throw Pelion* **upon Ossa,** *Ossa upon Pelion, and away with it.* This

1*

Book he has dedicated to his Patron *Julian*,
Secretary to the Muses, in hopes that he may get
and Under-Writer's Place somewhere about *Per-
nassus:* But alas! how can he ever hope for Preferment, when he has blasphem'd the best *Poet* of our
Age, by mistaking *Innocence* for *Ignorance:* I wish to
God the last may not rise up in Judgment against
him.   He (good Soul) is (as appears in his Epistle
to his Patron) for none of your high Flights; but,
like and humble Sinner in strict Diet, makes all his
Similies of *Cloose-Stools* with *Velvet Seats*, and *Pans*
that receive the Excrement.   God save us: What
are we when we are left to our selves.

  Now for his *Preface*, he would imitate that
ingenious one of Mr. *Dryden's* to *Ovid's Epistles*, in
beginning with *Ovid's* Life, which hath been wrote
by as many Men as there are *Lives* in *Plutarch*.
And again, our *Paraphraser* says, That *Ovid* was as
good a Wit as Himself, or any other Translator;
and, to prove that, he says, *Nescivit quod bene cessit*,
&c.   He might as aptly have said,

      The Man in the Moon drinks **Claret.**

  Then he says, That he could find no such thing
as *Clubbing* with *Ovid* in all the Catalogue of
Virgil, Catullus, Propertius or *Tibullus:* Very truly
said; for I suppose he knows nothing farther of
those Authors than the Catalogue.

Oh tempora! Oh Mores!
The more the merrier!

He wonders that so many Workmen should put their Shreds and Thrums together to dress *Ovid* in a *Buffoon's* Coat! why a silly Quaker, in plain *Taunton* Serge, thinks a Scarlet Coat embroider'd to be the *Old Serpent*.

He questions not but that there are more Fools in the World of his Opinion. (The true Question is, whether he is not single ᶠ)

Then he affirms, that, in his own simple naked Shape, he comes nearer the Original, than the best of 'em; when in *Sapho* to *Phaon* he begins at the sixth Distich, *Arva Phaon celebrat,* &c. and goes back to the fifth, *Uror ut in Domitis,* &c. leaving out the eight Verses preceding, by which you may easily guess that he had no other Authority for his *Paraphrase* (as he calls it) than the Translation: 'Tis something strange, that neither *Ovid* himself, nor Nineteen Judicious Translators, can give this Gentleman the least Hint or Light into *Publius Ovidius Naso's* Meaning.

Quo te mori pedes? ———

Now on a sudden he's started from Poetry, and is possest with the Spirit of sublunary Wealth, and wishes with all his Heart that he were as Rich as a *M.* or a *C.* then would he quit all his Title to *Pernas-*

sus, and engage never to write, oh, never to write
any more; that is to say, he'd be so unconscionable
as to have a good Estate for nothing :

> *God prosper long our Noble King*———

Now, as he says, the late Translators have
already clipp'd the Original, and why should not he
clip too : whereas my Fear is, he hath clipp'd *Ovid*
so close that it will hardly go :

> *When first King* Henry, &c.

I believe no Book hath had severer Usage than
our *Paraphraser's ;* for says he, it was hurry'd into
the Press before it cou'd make any Defence for it
self : Now the Meaning on't is, If it had met with
impartial Judges, it had never been Printed.

> *The Glories of our Birth and State*, &c.

But to conclude ; Having wonderfully shew'd his
Reading in his Preface to his aforesaid *Wits
Paraphras'd ;* in Scraps of old *Latin ;* and at last, to
his eternal Glory, one bit of false *Greek ;* he is so far
encourag'd, that he gives any Man a Challenge in
Chaldee, Arabick, and *Syriack*, though he confesses he
knows nothing of the matter : But, to try him, I'll
leave him with this *Syriack* Hexamiter.

> Erytit ut ælutap snabucer bus enimget igaf.

And to let you know that this last Verse, though

something rough, is not the effect of Indignation, I part friendly; only with this Advice, That our *Paraphraser* would consider, and follow any other Employment, more agreeable with his Genius (if he have any) than that of Poetry.

SAPHO to PHAON.

The ARGUMENT.

Sapho *was a Lady very Eminent for Singing of Ballads, and, upon an extraordinary Pinch, could make one well enough for her Purpose: She held a League with one* Phaon, *who was her Companion and Partner in the Chorus; but* Phaon *deserted his Consort, for the Preferment of a Rubber in the* Bagnio. *Sapho took this so to Heart, that she threatens to break her Neck out of a Garret-window; which, if effected, might prove her utter Destruction. Authors have not agreed concerning the Execution of her Design; but however she writes him this loving and terrifying Epistle.*

WHEN these my doggrel Rhimes you chance
      to see,
You hardly will believe they came from me;
'Till you discover *Sapho's* Name at bottom,
You'l not imagine who it is that wrote 'em.

2

I, that have often sung————*Young* Phaon *strove,*
Now sing this doleful Tune————*Farewel, my Love;*
I must not sing new Jiggs————the more's the pity,
But must take up with some old mournful Ditty.
You in the *Bagnio* have a Place, I hear;
I in my Garret sweat as much, with Fear :
You can rub out a Living well enough,
My Rent's unpaid, poor *Sapho* must rub off;
My Voice is crack'd, and now I only houl,
And cannot hit a Treble for my Soul.
My Ballads lye neglected on a Shelf,
I cannot bear the Burthen by my self;
Doll Price the Hawker offers very fair,
She'll sing along with me for Quarter-share ;
Sue Smith the very same will undertake ;
Their Voice is like the Winding of a Jack.
Hang 'em, I long to bear a Part with you,
I love to Sing, and look upon you too ;
Besides, you know when Songs grow out of fashion,
That I can make a Ballad on occasion.
I am not very Beautiful,————God knows ;
Yet you should value one that can Compose :
Despise me not, though I'm a little Dowdy,
I can do that—same—like a bigger Body :
Perhaps you'l say I've but a tawny Skin ;
What then ? you know my Metal's good within.
What if my Shoulder's higher than my Head ?
I've heard you say I'm Shape enough a-Bed:

The Mayor (God bless him) or the worthy Sheriffs
Do very often meet with homely Wives.
Our Master too, that little scrubbed Draper,
Has he not got a Lady that's a Strapper ?
If you will have a Beauty, or have none,
Phaon must lye—*Phaon* must lye alone.
I can remember, 'fore my Voice was broke,
How much in Praise of me you often spoke,
And when I shook a Trill, you shook your Ears,
And swore I sung like, what d'ye call 'em—Spheres :
You kiss'd me hard, and call'd me Charming Witch,
I can't do't now, if you wou'd kiss my Breach.
Then you not only lik'd my airy Voice,
But in my Fleshly Part you did rejoice ;
And when you clasp'd me in your brawny Clutches,
You swore I mov'd my body like a Dutchess ;
You clapp'd my Buttocks o'er and o'er again ;
I can't believe that I was crooked then.
Beware of him, you Sisters of the Quill,
That Sing at *Smithfield-Bars*, or *Saffron-Hill*,
Who, for an honest Living, tear your Throat ;
If *Phaon* drinks w'ye you're not worth a Groat :
And Ladies know, 'twill be a very hard Thing
To sink from him the smallest Copper-Farthing ;
Avoid him all—for he has us'd me so,
Wou'd make your Hearts ake, if you did but know.
My Hair's about my Ears, as I'm a Sinner,
He has not left me worth a Hood or Pinner.
2*

Phaon by me unworthily has dealt,
H'as got **my** Ring—though 'twas but Copper gilt ;
Yet that which vexes me,—Th'ungrateful Pimp
Has stole away my Petticoat with Gimp ;
H's all my Things; but, had he left me any,
I can't go out alone to get a Penny.
Phaon, **I** should have had less cause to grieve,
If, **like a** Man of Sense, you'd taken leave :
That **you'd** be gone, had I been ne'er so certain,
We might have drank a Pot or two at Parting :
Or fry'd some Bacon with an Egg ; or if
Into some Steaks we'd cut a Pound of Beef,
And laugh'd a while, that had been something like ;
But to steal off, was but a sneaking Trick.
My Landlady can tell, how I was troubled,
When I perceiv'd my self so plainly bubbled :
I ran like mad out at the Alley-Gate
To overtake you, but it was too late :
When I consider'd I had lost my Coat,
If I had had a Knife I'd cut my Throat ;
Yet notwithstanding all the Ills you did,
I Dream of you as soon as I'm in Bed ;
You tickle me, and cry, Do'st like it *Saff* ?
Oh wondrous well ! and then methinks I laugh.
Sometimes we mingle Legs, and Arms, and Thighs ;
Something between the Sheets, methinks does rise :
But when I wake and find my Dream's in vain,
I turn to Sleep only to Dream again.

When I am up, I walk about my Garret
And talk I know what—just like a Parrot :
I move about the Room from Bed to Chair,
And have no Satisfaction any where.
The last time I remember you lay here,
We both were dry ith' Night, and went for Beer ;
Into the Cellar by good Luck we got ;
What we did there, I'm sure you ha'n't forgot :
There stands, you know, an antiquated Tub,
'Gainst which, since that, I often stand and rub ;
Only to see't, as much Delight I take
As if the Vessel now were full of Sack ;
But more to add unto my Discontent,
There's been no Drink ith' Cellar since you went.
There's nothing but affords me Misery,
My Linnet in the Cage I fear will dye :
The Bird is just like me in ev'ry Thing ;
Like me it pines, like me it cannot sing.
Now *Phaon*, pray take Notice what I say,
If you don't bring the Things you took away ;
You know my Garret is four Stories high ;
From thence I'll leap, and in the Streets I'll die :
May be you will refuse to come—Do—do,
Y'had best let *Sapho* break her Neck for you.

Your afflicted Consort, Sapho.

PHILLIS to *DEMOPHOON:*

The ARGUMENT.

Demophoon *was born in* Holland, *who took after his Father* Theseus, *pretending to the Art of Piracy; he was cast upon* Newcastle-Shore *by adverse Winds (as the* Dutch *Commentators say) but we are inform'd he came hither by his own choice. No sooner arriv'd, but he heard that one* Phillis, *a single Woman, kept an Inn in the Town; There he took up his Quarters;* Phillis *observing him as a lusty Younker, and though his outward Habiliments were not very tempting; yet his Person persuaded her so far, that she Married him, and entrusted him with all. After some time, he told his Wife that his Occasions call'd him into* Holland *to see his Father, who he said was a Man of mighty Substance; He promised to Return within a Month, but hath not been heard of since. Therefore she writes to him this Letter; but whether it came to his Hands or no, hath been a Question to this Day.*

OUR Absence does discover your Disdain,
    You've done enough to make a Stone com-
        plain :
You told me you would stay a Month,—no more ;
But by my Nature I do find 'tis Four.
I, who am Woman, and a Lover too,
Observe the change of Moons, much more than you ;
Indisposition in the Head, or Back,
Informs our Sex beyond an Almanack.
Sometimes I hop'd—but soon that Hope did sink ;
Sometimes I thought—I knew not what to think.
I made my self a Liar———notwithstanding
There was no Ship—I swore I saw you Landing.
Some Curses on your Father I bestow,
That old *Dutch* Rogue, think I, won't let him go ;
But then again, that cannot likely seem,
The Maggot bites—you're gone away from him ;
What if you should be wrack't when hither bound ?
No,—you're too great a Villian to be drown'd.
Whom shall I blame ? whom but thy self-fond *Philly* ?
Wh' hast liv'd now Thirty Years, and art so silly.
When first you did within my Doors set footing,
I fell in Love,—forsooth—A Pox of Rutting ;
The Devil sure will have the Doctor *Hymen*,

Who told me, that his business was to try—men :
He did believe—you'd prove an honest Man.
Marry 'im, said he, with all the speed you can ;
The Good old Man, his Substance to increase,
Would match a Hell-hound to a Saint for Fees :
You swore such dreadful Oaths as ne'er were heard,
By th' *Belgick* Lyon, and the Prince's Beard ;
By *Opdam's* Ghost, and by the Dragon's Tail,
B' your Father's Head, and Mother's Farthingale ;
By the great Cannons, and the Bloody Flag,
And by the *Hogans Mogans* of the *Hague ;*
Your Execrations put m' in such a Fright,
That all the Hair about me stood upright :
If on your Head these Curses fall you've nam'd,
I must conclude, that certainly y'are damn'd.
Hearing such bloody Oaths, you would not stay,
I made all haste I could to get y'away :
I furnish'd you with all I cou'd afford,
Bisket and Powder'd Beef I put aboard ;
A Flask of Brandy to your Girdle hung,
Better I'm sure was never tipt o'er Tongue :
And when I patch'd your Sails with ancient Smock,
I thought they wou'd have brought me home good
    Luck ;
But stead of that—such was my Fatal **Hap,**
I prov'd the Instrument of your Escape.
When you came hither in a low Condition,
Did I not stuff your Gut with good Provision :
3

The Suit y'had on was destitute of Stitches,
I gave you then my Brother's Coat and Breeches;
But as for that—Pox on't—I'll ne'er repent it,
What you had wanted, I had then presented;
If you had never paid—here's none would stop ye;
But I must be your Wife too————like a Puppy:
I wish to God, that very Day we met,
That into Goal I had been thrown for Debt;
Then if I'd ask'd the Question————you'd have said,
Thank you, forsooth, I'm not in haste to Wed.
Well, well! Myn Hier! ye've caught me now 'tis true,
I hope I am the last you will undoe.
The *Dutch* by Paint describe each others Lives,
And draw their Neighbours Actions, and their Wives:
They'l draw your Father as some petty Pirate,
Doing small things, which People won't admire at.
He has been Rogue enough, but done no Wonders,
H'as robb'd a Fisherman of Eels and Flounders:
Perhaps he's drawn making a Sailor drunk,
Diving in's Pockets————to equip his Punk;
These are but Trifles to what you have done,
The Father's but a Coxcomb————to the Son:
You shall be Drawn, first in your tatter'd Cloaths,
Humbly complaining, full of Lies and Oaths;
And then you shall be Rigg'd from Head to Foot,
And from your Mouth this Label shall come out;
" Poor *Phillis*, of *Newcastle* upon *Tyne*————
" ' Twas I that ruin'd—now you see, I'm fine.

What must I do? I have not Trading here,
And all my Neighbours do but laugh and fleer;
One cryes, Where is your Husband *Demo*———foe?
For your right Name, not one of 'em does know;
Another cryes out———Hey! for *Amsterdam;*
What! Was'a *Dutchman, Phillis*———or a Sham?
Thus (as they say) they throw you in my Dish;
Wou'd I cou'd have you here but with a Wish,
For these Rogues sake; 'twould be good sport to see
How well you wou'd belabour two or three;
Then they'd change Tone, and cry—God bless ye
     both,
You are a handsom Couple, by my Troth:
No———'tis in vain to hope that you'l return,
I must continue, as I am, their Scorn.
But yet I can't forget the parting Day,
I thought you wou'd have hugg'd your Breath away;
At last you spoke—'twas this confounded Lye,
Phil, in a Month this o'er again we'll try;
But I believe that Trick you're trying now
With some tun-belly'd *Rotterdam*———*U'froe:*
If *Phillis* shou'd be talk'd on by the *Dutch*,
You'l say you never heard of any such.
Phillis! Who's she? Where does this *Phillis* dwell?
If you dont know, *Demophoon*, I'll tell;
" This is *Newcastle-Phillis*, she that did
" Once entertain you, Sir, at Board and Bed.
" Some small Remembrance *Phillis* hath deserv'd,

   3*

" Had not this *Phillis* been, you might have starv'd ;
" She gave you Mony, like a foolish Elf ;
" At last this *Phillis* gave away her—Self.
I am that *Phillis*, if I had my due,
That shou'd have Hang'd my self for Loving you :
It will not be too late to do it still,
And if I'm in a humour, 'faith I will.
Then on my Grave let these few Lines be writ,
Which *Phillis* made her self in Moody fit.

> *Here* Phillis *lyes ;*
> *Had she been wise,*
> S'*had Wed a Neighb'ring* Scotchman ;
> *And then she might,*
> *Have liv'd in spight*
> *Of any Drunken* Dutchman.

HYPERMNESTRA to LINUS.

The ARGUMENT.

There was lately a Gang of English *Highway-men, all of 'em having Wives or Whores in* London. *Now the only means to detect 'em, was by bribing their Women. In order to which the Keeper of* Newgate *went to 'em all, promising them very fairly, and withal using Arguments how serviceable they wou'd be to their Country, in discovering them; which they might easily do, when they came home to Bed. The Women were easily persuaded, and one Night order'd the Keeper to be there at such a time, who seized them all; but* Linus *was præadmonished by his Wife* Hypermnestra, *so he escap'd away in her Cloaths; She bore the brunt in his Apparel, and was taken (supposed to be a Man) and Committed to* Newgate, *and put into Irons. The rest of the Thieves were Hang'd, her Trial was respited, being not known who she was.* Hypermnestra *sends him this Letter.*

O thee poor *Hypermnestra* now complains,
Such is the Torture of my Iron Chains:

Shall it be call'd in Law, a Crime so heinous,
For being just to my own Husband *Linus?*
Let 'em Torment me on, I do not care,
I'll not tell who I am, nor where you are; ·
If they shou'd Hang me up instead of you,
To the last Gasp I swear I will be true;
I long to be reveng'd on those curs'd Wives,
That did betray their Friends and Husbands Lives.
Such Men were not in *England* to be found,
They'd bid the Devil stand, on any Ground;
And all the Prizes that they got, they spent
Upon these Whores; yet they were not content.
Think on that Night we did together Sup,
When all the Company were Cock-a-hoop;
That fatal Night you all came from the Pad,
Your Booty very large, your Hearts were glad:
Though in my sad Condition, 'tis not proper;
Yet, I can well remember all the Supper:
A stately Loin of Veal began the Feast,
I help'd you half the Kidney at the least;
Four Turkey-Pullets came next, you wish'd they'd
    been
Four *Turkey* Merchants upon *Mile-End-Green*.
Roasted young Ducks and Chickens fricazeed;
There was more Meat than we cou'd eat indeed:
Wine in abundance—I drank none but Sack,
But all you Men did ply it with Pontack:
To th' top you fill'd a Glass, and drank to th' best—
The Health, as you began it, seem'd a Jest;

I took't in earnest to my self, and knew
That I shou'd prove the best of Wives to you.
By Two a Clock you Men were almost Drunk,
Then each to bed went to his Spouse or Punk ;
If they were all as kind as you to me,
Never was such a Night of Lechery :
At last you sleep securely, without warning
Of the strange Alterations in the Morning.
I knew betimes the Keepers wou'd be there,
And all the Night I sweat, 'tween Sport and Fear :
At last I rose, and 'bout the Room I walk'd,
And thus at Random to my self I talk'd ;
Have I not sworn a Thousand Oaths at least,
That I'd betray my Husband with the rest ?
What must I do ? 'Tis true, I am his Wife,
What ! must I damn my Soul to save his Life ?
Hang all the Oaths in Christendom, said I ;
He is my Husband, and he must not die.
With that I drew your Breeches on in haste,
The Codpiece was so big, I was amaz'd ;
I walk'd into your Coat, hanging on Peg,
I lost my Head within your Perewig :
Having put on your Armour Cap-a-pee,
For by the Weight, such was your Cloaths to me ;
You reach'd your Arm across—had I been there,
You wou'd have had the other Bout, I fear ;
I pull'd the Sheet and Blanket from the Bed,
I plainly then perceiv'd, 'twas as I said :

Rise, *Linus*, Rise, said I, be very quick;
There is no time for any wanton Trick;
You're all betray'd——The Constable's at Door,
You must not stay a Minute of an Hour.
I shuffled on my Cloaths upon your Back,
They did not fit——I heard my Mantoe crack.
No sooner were you gone, but in they bounc'd;
They seiz'd on me, and swore I shou'd be trounc'd:
And here they have me fast with Bolt and Lock;
They know not yet that I have on a Smock.
Now you are safe, and I am here, dear *Linus*
Let's seriously discourse th' Affair between us:
If all the Truth to them I should discover,
What can they say? 'Twas acted like a Lover;
I may be sent to *Bridewel*, there they'll bang me,
But all the Law in *England* cannot hang me.
While I lye here——I am in little Ease,
But when all's told, what shall I do for Fees?
If you don't use some Means to get me freed,
Within few Days you'l hear that I am Dead;
And then 'tis like they'll bury me; if so
Upon my Grave this Epitaph bestow:

> *Here lies a Wife, who, rather than she'd fail*
> *To save her Husband's Life, dy'd in a Jayl.*

My Irons load me so, I'm fit to cry;
I wou'd write more, but cannot; so God b'ye.

HERMIONE to *ORESTES.*

The ARGUMENT.

Hermione *was the Daughter of* Menelaus and Helen :
Her Mother ran away with a young Fellow, one
Paris, *they went together beyond the Seas. Her
Husband, who lov'd her well, pursu'd 'em, and after
many Years found his Wife, and rescu'd her from
her Gallant, and without any Resentment of the
Injury took her again. During their Absence, their
Daughter (who had an Estate left her by her Unkle)
was committed to the Custody of her Grand-father,
who marry'd her to a School-fellow and Cousin-
German of hers, by name* Orestes. *Her Father
brought home with him one* Pyrrhus, *a wild young
Fellow, to whom he Marry'd her again, taking no
notice of the first Match. She, silly harmless Girl,
wonders at the Design, and to her husband* Orestes
writes this innocent Letter.

TO thee I write, my dear and only Cuz,
    Nor will I be afraid to call thee Spouse :

Though here's a Fellow come resolv'd to swear
I am his Wife, and he will make't appear:
He looks sometimes, as if he long'd to eat me,
Sometimes he looks so gruff, as if he'd beat me:
He says he is *Achilles* Son and Heir,
And bids me disobey him, if I dare;
He kisses me so hard, the strongest Man,
He gets a top of me do what I can;
With all my Strength my Legs together join,
But with one Knee he'll open both of mine.
I call him Rogue and Rascal, filthy Sot,
And all the beastly Names I can get out:
I'm Marry'd, Sirrah, therefore don't mistake it,
I have a Husband that will thwack your Jacket:
Yet that's all one, he cares not what is said;
But by the Hair he drags me into Bed.
They talk of Girls, forc'd by unruly Men,
They can't be forc'd so much as I have been:
Yet all this while *Orestes* comes not near me,
I am afraid you do not love your *Hermey*;
You'll fight for Mony, as you'd fight for Life,
And won't you fight a little for your Wife?
One while my Father mist my Mother *Helen*,
Lord! there was such a Noise, and such a Yelling,
He rais'd up all the People in our Lane,
And ne'er was quiet, 'till she came again.
I wou'd not have you make a Noise for me,
But come and kill this Fellow quietly;

Give him a good sound Blow, and never fear Man,
It is for me, your Wife and Cousin-German.
You know my Guardian marry'd me to you
When we were both so young, we cou'd not do—
Now from beyond Sea comes my Father huffing,
And will needs marry me to this same Ruffian ;
He vapours here about his Country Blood,
I guess your *English* Family's as good :
He says, you've led a very wicked Life,
And that you broke your Mother's Heart with Grief.
For talking so of you, I'd slit his Tongue,
And pull his Eyes out too, if I were strong.
'Tis something strange, we're of a Generation
Where Ravishing has been a mighty Fashion :
My Grand-mother was Ravish'd by one *Swan*,
A little Cousin by another Man :
My Mother has been Ravish'd once or twice ;
And I am Ravish'd now by her Advice.
Must I with such a Rogue as this be Match'd ?
A more unlucky Girl was never hatch'd.
My Mother left me here a little Wench,
Just big enough to clamber on a Bench ;
She was stark mad for that young Fellow—*Paris,*
And after him she danc'd the new Fagaries :
My Father for his Life cou'd not forbear,
But ran a Catter-wawling after her :
Now they're come Home, but with such alter'd Looks,
As if they were some strange Outlandish Fo'kes.
4*

My Father has a Beard below his Band,
I did not know my Mother, she so tann'd:
Toward my Good, what did she ever do?
When she was gone, I learn'd to Knit and Sew;
I use my Needle now as well's another,
But 'tis no God-a-mercy to my Mother:
When she came in, she knew not who I was;
This Girl, said she, is grown a strapping Lass,
She must be Marry'd, or she'll grow too busie;
Look here, I've brought thee home a Husband, Hussy;
With that he threw his Paws about my Neck;
Kill him, *Orestes*, or my Heart will break:
I draw the Curtains when he's fast asleep,
And out of Bed, soon as 'tis Day, I leap;
But I do toss and tumble all Night long,
As if by Bugs and Pismires I'd been stung:
Sometimes, when I'm asleep, by chance there lies
One of my Hands squeez'd close between his Thighs;
I snatch't away as soon as e'er I wake,
With as much speed, as if I had felt a Snake;
To t' other side o'th' Bed, I jerk from him,
And sometimes lay one Breech upon the Beam;
Then after me, he by degrees will steal,
Pray Sir keep off, say I, I am not well;
He seems as if he did not understand,
And then he reaches out his hasty Hand;
I speak as plainly to him as I can,
I tell him I'm not fitting for a Man.

Pshaw, pshaw! says he, I know you do but jest.
'Pon the whole matter, he's a filthy Beast.
For God's sake, *Orey*, prethee now contrive
Some way or other that he may not live :
For here I take my Oath upon a Book,
If you don't get me off by Hook or Crook,
That we may do as marry'd People may,
I'll either kill my self, or run away.

CANACE to MACAREUS.

Lately Translated out of

OVID;

Now BURLESQU'D.

The ARGUMENT.

Macareus *and* Canace, *Son and Daughter of Æolus (a Trumpeter of the Guards) being from Children brought up together, at the last grew so intimately acquainted, that they made bold to lye with one another.* Canace *prov'd with Child by her Brother* Macareus. *She was Deliver'd in the House; and the Nurse contrived to convey the Child through the Hall when* Æolus *was sounding his Trumpet, accompany'd with several sorts of Wind-musick; notwithstanding that Noise, the shrill Cry of the Infant was over-heard by* Æolus, *who sent it away to be left in the Streets, and expos'd to the Mercy of the Parish; and to his Daughter* Canace *he sent a Halter, with this Message,——This you have deserv'd,——and you know how to use it.* Canace *hang'd her self (as you may guess) before she wrote this Letter.*

EFORE these rude, distracted Lines you Read,
    Believe th' unlucky Authress of 'em Dead.
Ever to see me more's beyond all Hope,
One Hand a Pen, the other holds a Rope :
My blustring Father's troubled with a Whim,
And I must hang my self to humour him.

But when he sees my Carcase on the Floor,
Surely he'll cease to call me Bitch or Whore :
His puffing and his blowing will be in vain,
He cannot puff me into Life again :
His Mind is swell'd much bigger than his Face,
I am (he says) his Family's Disgrace :
All his great Friends and Kindred are provok'd ;
What are his Friends to [   ] when I am Choak'd ?
I wish that we had stifled one another
That Night I clung so closely to you, Brother :
Why did you love me more than did become ye ?
It had been happy, if y'ad kick'd me from ye :
When first, with Pleasure, I lay under you,
Would y'ad been lighter by a Stone or two.

At first I wonder'd what should be the Matter,
I look'd like Death, and was as weak as Water :
For sev'ral Days I loath'd the sight of Meat,
And ev'ry Night I chew'd the upper Sheet :
I'd such Obstructions, I was almost Moap'd,
My Breath came short, my———were stopp'd.

I call'd old Nurse, and told her how it was;
She, an experienc'd Bawd, soon groap'd the Cause:
Quoth she, for this Disease, take what you can,
You'll ne'er be well, 'till you have taken Man:
When I was Young, I thought I was bewitch'd;
I scratch'd my Belly, for it always itch'd.
The Truth I will no longer hide, said I,
I must enjoy my Brother, or I die:
She tickl'd me, and told me 'twas no Sin,
Nearer of Blood, said she, the deeper in:
Both you and I approv'd what Nurse had said;
So, without more a-do, we went to Bed:
You in my Belly rummag'd all about,
To find this wonderful Distemper out:
Too soon 'twould be discover'd, was my Fear,
I could have let you search'd for ever there:
But Nurse can tell how I did sigh and sob
When we perceiv'd that you had done the Job.

I made th' old Beldam foot it up and down
To ev'ry Quack and Mountebank in Town,
For *Dendelion*, and *Camelions-Thighs*,
Spirit of Saffron mixt with *Vultures Eyes*:
I would have given all I had been worth,
T' have kill'd the Child before it had come forth:
But the strong Rogue lay fencing in my Womb,
And did those pois'nous Potions overcome.
Oh! when I saw the Ninth Moon in the Wane,
Then I was in the Full——of Grief and Pain;
5

Then, then my Throws came on me thick and thick;
I groan'd, but for my Life I durst not shreik :
Until my Tortures came to such a Growth
That Nurse with both her Hands did stop my Mouth :
I should have cry'd so loud, that ev'ry Neighbour
Would have discover'd I had been in Labour:
No Woman yet that ever wore a Navel,
Endur'd so hard and so severe a Travel.

  I curs'd your Sex, and wish'd a Rot might come
On all the Stallions throughout Christen 'ome.
At last you came ; I knew you by your Tread ;
I peep'd at you, though I was almost Dead :
T' ward me you seem'd to have some kind Remorse,
But look'd, as if you would have eaten Nurse.

  You held my Back-Parts, you cou'd do no more ;
Would you had never felt the Parts before.

  Sister, said you, you shall not die this Bout,
We're both unlucky, but we'll rub it out.

  To see what Words from those we love can do !
(Surely the Child within me heard you too,)
For straight he sprang forth from me, and did seem
To make his Passage in a flowing Stream :
'Twas hard enough : But now's a harder Case,
To hide the Business from my Father's Face ;
We did consult how to devise a Way
Thorough the Hall our Bastard to convey.

  My Father in Wind-Musick still delighted,
And all the Gang that Night he had invited :

Fellows that play on Bag-Pipes, and the Fife;
The old Man always lov'd a noiseful Life:
They all did Sound together after Supper,
And then to carry him off, we thought, was proper.

Nurse in her Apron took the little Brat,
Swath'd up in Linnen, Rushes over that;
Quite through the Hall she went her usual Pace,
And, unconcern'd her self, humm'd *Chevy-Chase.*

Just to the Door she'ad safely carry'd him,
When the unlucky Wretch began to screme:
His little Organ made a shriller Noise
Than all the Flutes, Recorders, and Ho-boies:
The old Man prick'd his Ears up, like a Hare,
And after Nurse ran nimbly as the Air:
Whither so fast, said he, old Mother Trundle?
Pray, let us see, what have you in your Bundle?
Quoth Nurse,—'Tis Mistress *Canny's* dirty Smock,
Men into Womens Secrets should not look.

He puff'd away the Rushes from her Lap,
And there appear'd the little sprawling Ape:
'Zounds, says my Father, What is here? A Kid!
My Daughter *Canny's* finely brought to Bed?

He rais'd so great a Tempest in the House,
I thought that Hell it self was broken loose;
He rag'd so loud, the Bed shook under me;
Methought I was in some great Storm at Sea:
He rush'd into the Room, and did discover
The bloody Symptoms of a Child-bed Lover:

5*

Our Sexes Stains by him were here descry'd,
Which Women from their own dear Husbands hide :
With his own Hands he did design to wound me,
But that he saw something like Murther round me :
The Bastard in the Streets he did expose,
And what will be his Destiny„ God knows :
The little Knave, with Tears, did seem to answer,
As who should say, I beg your Pardon Grandsire,
Out went old *Trump ;* I by his Looks could find
There was some Mischief hatching in his Mind.

In came a Fellow of the *Bag-Pipe* Gang,
Whose very Whiskers seem'd to say, Go hang ;
Before his Words came out his Tongue did falter ;
At last he spoke, *Canny*, look here's a Halter :
Your Father says, 'Tis this you do deserve ;
If you'll not use it, you may live and starve.
His most obedient Daughter he shall think me ;
If I don't hang my self, the Devil sink me.

Since Whoring does produce such strange Effects,
Would I'd been born a Monster without Sex :
Let my young Sisters all be warn'd by me,
And curb betimes incestuous Lechery.

This I request of you, dear Brother *Mac,*
That of our wretched Child some Care you'd take ;
If you can find him out, be not unwilling
Towards his Maintenance to drop a Shilling.

Let these my last Words be observ'd by you,
As I obey my Father's:——so,—Adieu.

ARIADNE to *THESEUS*,

Lately Translated out of

OVID;

Now BURLESQU'D.

The ARGUMENT.

Theseus, *an English Gentleman, and one who for his Diversion admir'd Travelling*, especially on Foot, *having safely arriv'd at* Calais, *walk'd on easily from thence to* Paris, *where he had not long been but he receiv'd an unmannerly Justle from a Cavalier of* France: Theseus, *whose great Soul could not brook the least Affront, resented this so highly, that he challeng'd him, fought him, and after a long and skilful Dispute between 'em, fairly kill'd him:* Theseus *was imprison'd in the* Bastile; *During his Restraint he held a League with* Ariadne, *the Keeper's Daughter: And, though the Prison was as diffi-cult as a Labyrinth, (such is the Power of Love,) she soon contriv'd a way for his Escape by Night: and he, accompany'd with Mistress* Ariadne, *footed it back to* Calais; *where, both lodging together at*

the Red-Hart, *he very unkindly took the Advantage of*
her Snoaring, and stole from her early in the
Morning; and went off with the Pacquet-Boat to
Dover; *from whence he gently walk'd to* London:
Ariadne *sends him These.*

NO savage *Bear*, no *Lion*, *Wolf*, or *Tyger*,
    Would ever use his Mistress with such Rigor;
D'ye think you don't deserve ten Thousand Curses,
For leaving me in Pawn at Monsieur *Forces ?*
I wonder what the Tavern People think !
For **here I sit**, and dare not call for Drink.
While by your side I innocently lay,
You might have taken leave a civil Way:
I was half waken'd from a pleasant Sleep
By th' melancholy Sound of *Chimney-sweep :*
I stretch'd my Leg, to find out my Bed-fellow,
But I could groap out nothing but the Pillow;
Thinking t' have hugg'd you in my Arms so close,
One of the Bed-staffs almost broke my Nose:
Thes. Thes. said I, I hope you are not gone:
I might as well have call'd the Man i' th' Moon:
I rent my Head-cloaths off, *mortdieu ! mortdieu!*
What will become of me!   What shall I do ?
I op'd the Casement as the Morning dawn'd ;
And then could plainly see that I was pawn'd.
With calling you I tore my Throat to pieces,
The Eccho jeer'd me with the Name of *Theseus :*

To th'top of all the House I ran undrest:
The People thought that I had been Possess'd:
At last, I spy'd you in the Pacquet-Boat;
I knew 'twas you, or so at least I thought:
Had you been walking, I had known your Stride,
And guess'd your Strut from all Mankind's beside:
Both Seas and Winds must needs be kind to thee,
Thou art so like 'em in Inconstancy.
I thump my Breast, I Rage, I Storm and Fume;
The House desires I would discharge my Room:
Quoth one o'th' Servants, Mistress *Ariadne*'s
Past all Recovery, overwhelm'd with Madness:
Another crys, *Mam'sell Com' portez vou'?*
Fetch me my *Thes.* said I, What's that to you.
When in the Boat I cou'd no longer see you,
Ten Thousand De'ils of Hell, said I, go wi' you.

  They think I'm Drunk, I'm sure 'tis not with Wine;
The Score's too large; and you have left no Coin.
Into a Corner I am sometimes dogg'd,
And there I Cry as if I had been Flogg'd:
Sometimes I roul my self upon the Bed,
And act those Postures o'er that once we did:
To my own self with Pleasure I repeat,
Here lay my Head, and there I put my Feet:
I often call to Mind our am'rous Work;
Then here, methinks I have you with a Jerk.
Sometime they talk, that Ships are safe at home:
I listen then, to hear if you are come.

Were I a Man, into the Seas I'd douse,
And after you I'd Swim, and bilk the House:
If I should offer to run home again,
My Father'd keep me in an Iron Chain;
I have betray'd the old Man's Trust for you;
I may go whistle for a Portion now:
When, for your Sake, I stole the Prison Keys,
I little thought to see such Days as these:
Oh! when you Love was mounted to a Pitch,
You hugg'd me as the Devil hugg'd the Witch;
You swore with Oaths most desperate and bloody
The Queen of *France* to me was but a Dowdy.
I have more Whymsies than a dancing *Bear*,
Sometimes I dream the Constable is here:
And though the Waiters very often wheedle,
Yet I suspect that they will bring the Beadle.
Again, I fear they'll spirit me away,
And send me Slave into *Virginia:*
I was not bred a Drudge from the beginning,
Except it were to wash my Father's Linnen.

Either to Sea or Land I durst not look,
To Heav'n I can't; you've stole my Prayer Book:
Your Valour made my Fortune so untoward,
I would to God that you had been a Coward:
Distressed *Ariadne* now complains,
Because such sprightly Blood runs in her Veins:
They say we *French* are very Hot, 'tis true;
But yet our Sparks are Frost and Snow to you:

Curst be the time when you first learn to Fence,
(Though that does never alter Men of Sense.)
   I fancy in what Posture you were found,
One Foot heav'd up, the other on the Ground :
As much of Warlike Grace you did discover
As any *Roman* Statue in the *Lovre*.
Methinks I hear you speak to th' Cavalier,
Sa ! Sa ! Monsieur, I have you here and there :
But now your valiant Acts are lost for ever,
By sneaking off, like a *French-Ribbon-Weaver*.
   Had I not drank that *Brandy* over Night,
I cou'd have wak'd, and so have stopp'd your Flight.
Curst be the Wind which was so kind to you ;
Curst be the Boat, and curst be all its Crew ;
Curst may I be for trusting what you said,
Curst may all Lovers be that Snore in Bed.
Poor *Ariadne*, thou art finely serv'd,
Thy too much Love has brought thee to be starv'd :
The Servants pity me, and say't's a hard case,
I've nothing here to pay 'em with but Carcase :
This Carcase too has wept out all its Juice,
'Tis grown so dry, 'tis fit for no Man's use.
Think, when you're rev'ling in your Cups at *London*,
That your Poor *Ariadne* here is undone,
And when you come where People do resort,
To hear your Travels told were pretty Sport :
With what rough Bit of Flesh you did engage ;
You thought you should be killing him an Age:
6

Do not forget me when you tell your Tale,
Tell'em how I releas'd you out of Goal:
And how with you **I stole** on Foot through Alleys;
And, pray forget not, that I'm pawn'd at *Calais :*
And, when this Tale **to** your Companions told,
Imagine *Ariadne* Stiff and Cold:
When Dead, they'll bury me in some back Garden,
For I can't give the Parish Clerk a Farthing.

    And 'tis for you I all these Sorrows prove;
So, Mr. *Theseus*, thank you for your Love:

LEANDER to HERO.

The ARGUMENT.

Leander *an Usher of a School, and chief Poet of* Richmond, *having contracted a more than ordinary
Acquaintance with Mistress* Hero *of* Twitnam,
*a Governess or Tutress to young Ladies; such a
reverential Esteem had they procur'd to themselves
at each Place, that they could not conveniently meet
without great Scandal; therefore the Usher frequently
Swam over to his Mistress by Night, but at this time
the* Thames *was so rough, that he was constrained to
convey his Mind to* Hero *by a Waterman in these
Poetical Lines, wherein Love and Learning strive to
outvie each other.*

YOUR faithful Lover sends this Bille'dou'x.
Stuff'd full of Love, but not a Word of News.
Believe not, I think much of any Labour,
Cou'd I have come my self, I'd nere' sent Paper;
6*

The *Thames* is rough, the Winds so hard do blow,
I scarcely got a Waterman to go.
And **if I** wou'd have giv'n a Thousand Pound,
This was **the** only Fellow to be found.
I stood upon the Shoar while he went off,
The Boat once gone, I thought 'twas well **enough.**
I must **be** careful whom I send by Water,
Our Family begins to smoak the Matter:
Just as the Letter went, I had a fancy
Came in my Head, I cou'd have made a Stanza:
Go Paper, go, and kiss a whiter Hand,
That oft hath put *Leander* to a stand.
Methinks the Nymph perfumes it with her Breath,
And bites the Wax off with her Iv'ry Teeth:
Her Shepherd would be glad to be so bit,
Until th' aforesaid Teeth together met.
But then, think I, those Whymsies she'll condemn,
The Hand that writes, should rather make me Swim:
Bold Strokes in Poetry she hardly blames,
But such bold Stroaks should be upon the *Thames:*
Methinks it is an Age since I swam o'er,
I long until each Arm does prove an Oar.
Fully resolv'd I came to'th Water-side,
And thought the Space between us but a Stride.
I saw your House, and wish'd that I cou'd clamber
To your Watch-Light in the supremest Chamber:
I pull'd off Coat and Doublet twice or thrice,
But then I thought,—be Merry and be Wise.

Thus I in Verse spake to the mighty *Boreas*,
Thou blustring Youth —pray tell me why so furious;
Tho' amongst Winds thou art a great Commander,
Blow gently for the sake of poor *Leander*.
I cross no Sea (Here *Thames* is call'd the Sea,
Because it doth with lofty Verse agree.)
I cross no Sea to *Asia* or to *Africk*,
Upon th' Account of Sublunary Traffick:
Ingots of Gold I alas I do not seek 'em,
Give me my *Hero's* Love, then *omnia mecum*.
Boreas himself does sometimes leave off roaring,
And goes a Woing, I'll not say a Whoring.
For sev'ral uses you your Breath may spare,
Do not so fiercely move our *Richmond* Air.
But all was vain, *Boreas* was still unkind;
I did repeat my Verses to the Wind.
Had I but Wings, I'd soar above the People
And place my self just now on *Twitnam* Steeple.
I well remember the first Night I Swam,
That happy Night I first to *Twitnam* came;
I put off all my Cloaths, with them my Fears,
And dous'd into the *Thames* o'er Head and Ears.
The Moon took care *Leander* should not sink,
And stole before me like a lighted Link:
I thank'd her for her Love, and thus did greet her,
As far as my poor Talent went in Meeter:
Ah gentle Moon, because thou'rt kind to me,
I wish *Endymion* may be so to thee:

And as with him thou hold'st a private League,
With thy broad Eye, so wink at my Intrigue.
Under Correction to your Heav'nly Sense,
Your Case and mine have little Difference.
A Goddess you love one of human Birth,
My Mistress is a Goddess upon Earth:
Such sort of Beauty as she wears, is giv'n
Only to such as do belong to Heav'n.
And if you are not of the self same Mind,
Begging your Pardon, *Cynthia,* you're Blind.
With such like Words I got near *Twitnam* Sands,
And nothing all the Way saw I but Swans.
At last I spy'd your Candle on the top,
Ay! now all's well, thought I, there is some Hope.
But when you put your Head out of the Cazement,
Then was *Leander* struck into Amazement;
For two Lights more did from the Window seem,
Which made the Artificial one look dim.
Your Eyes, the Moon and Candle made just four;
I, like some Prince was lighted to the Shoar.
But you're to blame, when you perceiv'd me come,
Nurse says, she could not keep you in the Room,
But in your Shift you wou'd be running down;
You'll get some violent Cold, and then you're gone.
But to say Truth, thou art a loving Tit,
Thou hug'st me in thy Arms all dropping Wet:
I can but think how strangely I did look,
When you put o'er my Head a Holland Smock;

And Hand in Hand thus walking from the *Thames*,
We seem'd the Ghosts of two Distressed Dames.
But when we came to Bed, we understood
We were no Ghosts, but real Flesh and Blood:
We did repeat more Pleasure in one Hour,
Than some dull Lovers do in Forty-score,
Because we knew our Time was very short,
We cou'd not tell the Number of our Sport.
Aurora does from *Tithon's* Bed escape,
Tithon perhaps would take the other Nap,
See her Postilian *Lucifer* before,
And now the Bus'ness of the Night is o'er;
The Day appears, *Leander* must be jogging,
And home again among the Boys a flogging.
My well beloved *Amo* I forsake,
And to dull *Doceo* now I must go back.
A Substantive I'll always be to thee,
My pretty Verb *Deponent* thou shalt be.
If we were in Conjunction Day and Night,
Leander would not prove a Heteroclite:
In Grammer we make Noun to join with Noun,
Why shou'd not *Twitnaum* join with *Richmond* Town?
'Twou'd make one mad to think a foolish River,
Or any surly Winds should Lovers sever:
But hold *Leander*, let not Seas nor Wind
Disturb the quiet Freehold of thy Mind.
When first I crost—methought the Fish did gaze,
The Salmon seem'd to peep upon my Face;

I could hear Boatmen call from Western Barge,
What Fish is that, methinks 'tis very large :
They'd call me Porpus, and they'd jeer and flout me ;
But now by th' Name of Brother they salute me :
How d'ee says one ; Good morrow t'other cryes ;
I civilly return them, *Bona dies.*
The Fisherman that bobs all Night for Eel,
Now says, Your Servant, Sir, I wish you well :
God send you safe on t'other side the Water.
I say unto him, *Salvus sis Piscator.*
I hope those Halcyon Nights will soon return ;
For want of 'em, does poor *Leander* mourn.
But if such Storms in Summer time does hinder,
How shall I e'er get to thee in the Winter ?
If I do venture in, and should be drown'd,
I hope by thee my Body will be found.
Thou'lt roul it up in Holland or in Bucram,
Then may I truly say—*Mors mihi Lucrum.*
But let not this possess you I am dead,
A foolish Whimsey came into my Head.
We shall have many pleasant Nights between us,
I'll come and hugg my *Hero ore-tenus.*
Pray put these Lines up safe, for fear you loose 'em,
In that warm Place where I would be, your Bosom :
And in a little time, dispute it not
I'll come and justifie what I have wrote :
For when the Weather changes I'll not fail ye,
And until then thou—*dulce decus Vale.*

HERO's *ANSWER.*

Eander, thank you kindly for your Letter,
   Though if y'ad come your self it had been
      better;
I cannot rest, I know not what's the matter,
I'm all a-fire, to have you cross the Water.
We Women, when we've any thing to do,
Are ten times more desirous of't than you;
Having dismist your little Boys from School,
You can walk out i'th' Ev'ning when 'tis cool;
You can divert your self a hundred Ways,
I only stand upon the Shoar, and gaze;
You have a Green in which you Boul, or Bett,
And now and then three or four Shillings get;
Or to the Tavern, when you please you go,
And drink a Bottle with a Friend or so;
While I sit moap'd—like a neglected Cat,
And now and then with old dry Nurse I chat:
What's your Opinion, Nurse, and tell me truly,
D'ye think the Wind to Night will be unruly?
7

What, will *Leander* come ? or keep away ?
Faith I don't know, says she, 'tis like he may.
Such drowsie Answers I do seldom miss,
D'ye think I han't a blessed Time of this ?
Up to my Chamber, when 'tis Night, I get,
And in the Window is my Candle set ;
Perhaps I read a Play, or some Romances,
I soon grow weary of such Idle Fancies :
Then I peruse your Letter o'er again,
And more and more admire your learned Strain ;
Then I ask Nurse's Judgment in the case,
But she, old Soul's, as dull as e're she was ;
I make her stand upright (there I mistake,
She can't stand so—for sh' as a huckle Back)
I mean, I set her somewhere in the Room,
And she's to act as it you just were come ;
My only Joy (say I) thou'rt welcome hither,
How didst thou Swim to me this stormy Weather ?
Speak, let me hear some Musick from thy Mouth,
Nurse nods, and says—I'm pretty well forsooth :
Thus I beguile the time 'till Morning peep,
Then I go into Bed, and fall asleep.
And there I do enjoy you in my Dreams,
Spite of the Devil, or the rougher *Thames*.
Methought I saw yon come start [stark] naked in,
Wet were your Locks, and dropping was your Skin,
I with an Apron rubb'd you up and down,
And dry'd you from the Toe unto the Crown ;

Then presently we hugg'd with such a force,
I shook the Bed, and wak'd and startled Nurse;
And finding it to be a Dream—no more,
I grew as Melancholy as before.
If in a Dream such tickling Joys appear,
Much pleasanter 'twou'd be, if you were here.
I don't know what to think; you us'd to say,
Ten Thousand Devils should not stop your Way.
Why should the Danger at this Time be more?
The Wind blows hard, and so it did before;
But now I see which Way 'tis like to drive,
A *Richmond* Wench as sure as I'm alive;
Ah! say ye so? why then it is for her
This Storm is rais'd, *Leander* cannot stir.
But hang't that cannot be, I'm turn'd a Fool,
Leander was and is an honest Soul.:
As soon as I had said these Words of you,
The Candle burn't not as it us'd to do;
Says Nurse, there is a Stranger in the Light,
Master *Leander* will be here to Night;
With that she took the Brandy-bottle up,
And pulled from thence a very hearty Sup,
Says she—if what I say should prove untrue,
I wish this blessed Draught may ne'er go through;
Therefore let's see you here to Night, dear *Nandy*,
Or else poor Nurse must never more drink Brandy.
Perhaps you fancy you take double Pains,
And make too great a Trespass on your Reins,
7*

To Swim so far as you have us'd to do,
And after that to please a Mistress too;
Half of one half I'd ease you if I cou'd,
And meet you in the middle of the Flood;
But from the latter Service never flinch,
I should be loath to bate you half an Inch;
But after all, excusing what I'ave said,
Pray do not cross the River Hand o'er Head;
I dream't last Night, I hope 'tis no ill Luck,
A Spaniel Dog was hunting of a Duck,
There were some Reads which under Water grew,
And more, perhaps, than the poor Spaniel knew.
He was intangled there, and there was found,
I came to help him, but the Curr was drown'd.
I do not tell this Dream to make you **tardy,**
But as a **Caution** not to be fool-hardy.
The Wind will soon be laid, the *Thames* **be clear,**
Then you may cross it, without Wit or Fear;
Make much of this, for if you fail me, then,
By all the Gods I'll never write again.

LAODAMIA to PROTESILAUS,

Lately Translated out of

OVID;

Now BURLESQU'D.

The ARGUMENT.

In the War between England *and* Holland, *one* Pro-
tesilaus, an English *Lieutenant of a Fifth Rate
Frigat, being Wind-bound upon the* Downs; *his Wife*
Laodamia, *hearing he was not gone off, sent him this
Letter ; and, like a fond Wife, gives him strict Caution
to avoid Fighting.*

A Health to your Prosperity goes round,
   And to your safe Return before you're
      drown'd :
My Neighbour *Jackson*'s Wife began it to me ;
If I don't wish it, may it ne'er go through me :

We drink, and fancy to our selves in vain,
That the good Winds will blow him back again.
I hate the Noise of a tumultuous Sea,
Give me a Tempest rais'd by you and me ;
A Storm in which all Parts about us shake,
When we can hear the Bed beneath us crack.
At *Gravesend*, when we took our last Adieu,
The parting Kiss, remember, I gave you :
I, like a shitten Girl, began to cry ;
I had no Mind, methoughts, to say, God b'w'y :
I heard Tarpaulins roar out, Hoise up Sail ;
On Board, on Board ; here comes a merry Gale.
In such brisk Gales poor Women don't delight,
They blow away the Pleasures of the Night.
As you went off, I could not bear the Loss,
A Qualm came o'er my Stomach quite a-cross :
Old Mother *Crump*, a very subtile *Croan*,
Saw by my Looks that I was almost gone :
A Pint of Brandy presently she brought,
And made me drink a very hearty Draught ;
She shew'd her Love, but what great good has't done ?
How can I live with Comfort now you're gone ?
I wake, and find no Husband by my Side ;
I often think 'twere better I had dy'd :
'Till you return, I'll ne'er be drest again ;
I have not Comb'd my Head the Lord knows when :
A Glass of Wine sometimes my Heart does cherish ;
Wer't not for that, I fancy I shou'd perish :

Because I go so taudry, like a Punk,
Some, that don't know me, think that I am Drunk:
My Neighbours often tell me, Mistress *Protes,*—
You go so strangely, all the Street takes notice !
Says one, You do your Husband's Friends disgrace ;
For shame ! Put on a Petticoat with Lace :
Why should they think that I would wear a lac'd-
    Coat,
When my poor Husband's in a Sea-man's Wast-coat ?
Should I adorn my Head with Curles and Towers ?
When a poor Skippers Cap does cover yours.
   The Plaguy *Dutch ;* that they should break the
    Peace,
And not submit to us in *English* Seas :
Though, for my own particular, I swear,
If I could once again but have you here,
Let *Dutch* have Liberty fish and fowl,
I would not care a Farthing, by my Soul.
Methinks I see you now, and, by your Looks,
You are engaging with a Butter-box :
Methinks just now a Bullet did escape,
And hit my Neck, just in the very Nape.
But oh ! I swoon, when I do think of *Trump !*
His Ships now giving yours a bloody Thump !
Bless us, said I, Now you are dispatch'd !
That Dog has been at Sea 'fore you were hatch'd :
For Heav'ns sake avoid him if you can,
He's certainly the Devil of a Man !

If any Ship does **make** up towards you,
You may say sure *Van Trump*'s among the Crew :
There's not a Shot does to your Vessel come,
But I **receive** the Pain on't here **at home.**
What am I better if you beat the *Dutch*,
And you come hither hopping on a Crutch ?
How finely 'mong the Neighbourhood 'twould show,
To see you **strut** upon a **Timber Toe** ?
To rout the Foe is some great Adm'ral's Office,
In these Engagements you are but a Novice :
Your single Valour's nothing on the Sea,
Your Combat should be Hand **to** Hand with me.
Would I were in the Fleet **with** *Trump* **or** *Ruyter*,
To them I would become an Humble Suitor,
And **point** out to them where your Squadron lay,
Directing **them to shoot** another Way :
I'd speak **t'em** thus : Great Souls of *Amsterdam*,
Pray hear **a** silly Woman, as I am ;
And let your Cannon my poor Husband shun,
He knows not to discharge a little Gun :
If **you were** Women, as you're Warlike Men,
He would perform great **Actions wi'** you then :
Your Fighting, Skirmishing, **and** breaking Bones,
Are only fit for Men that want their Stones.

   Just as you were commanded to your Ship,
Remember, **at the** Stairs your Foot did slip ;
Think on that Slip, and, when the *Dutch* are shooting,
Duck down **your** Head, as if you wanted footing.

I wish your Captain some good Coward were,
And durst not bring the Vessel up for Fear:
I wish to God he would not sail too fast;
You'll come too soon, although you come the last.
When you return, they'll ask how Matters stand;
I hope you'll know no more than we at Land.

   All the Day long I smell no Scent but Powder,
Each Minute Guns go louder off and louder.
Most marry'd Women long 'till it be Night,
But, for my part, I hate the Thoughts of it;
Unless, by chance, I sleep, and Dream of you:
Fancy's the kinder Husband then o'th' two:
And when I wake and feel the Linnen wet,
I find I've Wept for Joy upon the Sheet:
This to Enjoyment gives but half Content;
When shall we meet together by Consent?
Oh, how I long to hear you tell in Bed
Some strange Romantick Tale of what you did!
But when you find you can't prolong the Jest,
And, being at a *Stand,*—kiss out the rest.

   Against both Wind and Tide why will you go?
You'd scarce come home if Wind and Tide said no.
You fight, methinks, about so mean a Thing,
Which should have Privilege of catching *Ling :*
Old-Ling I hate worse than a common Whore;
(Would you lov'd Fighting with the *Dutch* no more:)
I eat it once, and that against my Will,
And sometimes fancy that I smell on't still.
  8

But though thou art expos'd to Seas and Wind,
It is some Ease unto my troubled Mind
To see thy comely Picture in the Hall,
Drawn to the Life with Charcoal on the Wall :
I prattle to it as if thou wert here ;
'Tis late, Pr'ythee lets go to Bed, my Dear :
Methinks thou say'st, I'll humour thee for once ;
Thoul't work me at the last to Skin and Bones :
I kiss the Wall, and do my Cheeks besmear,
And ope my Mouth, as if your Tongue was there.
By all the pleasant Postures of Delight,
By all the Twines and Circles of the Night,
By the first Minute of our Nuptial Joys,
When you put fairly for a Brace of Boys,
I do conjure you, have a special Care,
And let not saucy Danger come too near ;
For when I hear that thou art knock'd o'th' Head,
I'll hold you ten to one that I am dead.

OENONE to PARIS.

The ARGUMENT.

Paris *was the Son of* Priam *a Wealthy Old Citizen and Alderman of* London. *When* Hecuba *his Mother was big with Child of him, she dreamt a foolish conceited Dream, which occasion'd Old* Priam *to consult* Lilly, *who told him, That* Paris *in process of time would occasion his House to be burnt down. Therefore the credulous Alderman sends him into the Country far* North *to be dispos'd of as a By-blow. When he grew fit for Service he was entertain'd in a Gentleman's House, where he contracted a Bosom-acquaintance with* OEnone *a young Wench and fellow-Servant with him in the same House. His Father began to come to himself, and hearing where he was, sent for him, and own'd him as his Son; but before that he had disengag'd himself from Service, and ran away with one* Hellen, *who was Wife to* Menelaus. OEnone *being inform'd of all these Proceedings, writes to him this Letter.*

Fter my hearty Love to you remember'd,
    Hoping you are not in Body distemper'd.

8*

More than my self at the Writing hereof,
If it be so, we are both well enough:
Your Usage has been such to poor *Oenone*,
That none but such a Fool as I would own ye;
I hear you're run away with *Menel's* Wife,
I pity her, she'll lead a blessed Life;
What mighty Mischief have I done, I wonder;
You'll never have a younger, nor a sounder.
If by my means y'had met with some Disaster,
Had I procur'd you Anger from your Master;
If I had giv'n you that they call a Clap,
You'd had some small Excuse for your Escape:
But now you've had your Ends, away to sneak,
Come! come! these things would make a body speak.
You were not then so uppish—when you said,
A Dutchess was a T—— t' a Servant Maid;
You were a Groom your self, you know 'tis truth,
Not all your Greatness now—can stop my Mouth;
If you were able to keep House you swore
You'd marry me, for all I was your Whore.
We were together on a Summers Day,
Both in the Stable, on a Truss of Hay;
You can't forget some pretty Pastimes there,
No body saw us but the Chesnut Mare:
You said such glorious Things, the very Beast
Prick'd up her Ears, and thought you were in Jest:
But I did prove the verrier Beast o'th' two,
For like an Ass I thought that all was true:

Soon after—you were taken from the Stable,
To wait upon your Master at his Table ;
To undertake it you seem'd very loath,
Did I not teach you then to lay a Cloath ?
There's no Man but must have his first Beginning,
Who learnt you then to fold your Table-Linnen ?
Did you not often when the Cloath was spread,
Just in the middle put your Salt and Bread ?
You have been threaten'd oft to loose your Place,
Because you knew not how to fill a Glass ;
You pour'd in Wine up to the very top,
I told you you should fill but to the Knob.
Did I not shew you how to broach your Drink,
And tilt the Vessel when't began to sink ?
I was your dearest Honey—all that while
There was not such a Girl in forty Mile :
You carv'd my Name upon the Trencher-Plates,
And on the Elms before the outward Gates ;
And as we see in time those Elms encrease,
So will my Name grow greater with the Trees ;
And any one that stands but at the Door,
May see *Oenone* (your obedient Whore.)
You never have been well, since those three Maids,
Rather those impudent and bold-Fac'd Jades
Differ'd among themselves, which it should be
That had the cleanliest Shape of all the Three.
To you they came when you were in the Close,
The little Field that was behind the House,

Stark Naked did they come from Top to Toe,
Paris, say they, we will be Judg'd by you.
Heav'ns preserve your Eye-sight, how you gaz'd!
Nor could you speak a Word, you were so maz'd;
At last you judg'd, with many a hum! and haw!
Venus the finest Wench that e'er you saw.
This was a *Whitson* Frolick, as they said,
A pretty Prank to shew you all they had.
To see how naked Women are betwitching,
Since that y'have minded nothing else but bitching.
Soon after that your Project was of stealing
That over-ridden Whore, that Mistress *Hellen.*
I must be gone a little while, you said,
(Then was this Bus'ness brooding in your Head.)
You kist me hard as if I cou'd not feel,
And swore that you wou'd be as true as Steel:
Said you—Doubt nothing, for the Case is plain,
I'm prov'd the Son of an Old Alderman,
And sent for home, my Father's very ill,
I must be by, at making of his Will;
Oh that we cou'd but bury the old Cuff,
Then marry you, all wou'd be well enough.
You may've a richer Wife, but not a better,
For I am no such despicable Creature:
Not to disparage your good Lady Mother,
I can behave my self as well's another.
No Wife like me was there in Christendom,
When you were honest *Pall*—Squire *Sheephard's* Groom.

My Father's but a plain Old Man, 'tis true,
But's Daughter has been bred up as high as you.
He is an honest Man, whatever I am,
And may be sav'd as soon as Master *Priam*.
Were I your Wife my Carriage shou'd not shame
Your Mother *Hec*,—tho' she's a stately Dame.
What though these Hands have us'd a Drippin-Pan,
Yet on Occasion they can furl a Fan.
Now on a little folding Bed I lye,
(Tho' in that Bed sometimes lay you and I)
Yet I know how perhaps to hold my Head,
If I were carried to a Damask Bed.
If you had marry'd me y'had met with Quiet,
What can y'expect from her but Noise and Riot?
You now have caught a most notorious Strumpet;
Besides 'tis known, as if y'ad blown a Trumpet:
Where e're you come you'll meet with Frumps and
    Jeers,
Her Husband too will be about your Ears.
In little time from you she will be budging,
She'll lye with any Body for a Lodging.
When first of all we closely were acquainted,
(Which now it is too late, I have repented)
Cassandra was a Gipsey in the Town,
Who went a Fortune telling up and down;
I gave her broken Meat, which we cou'd spare,
She'd tell me all my Fortune to a Hair:
You love (says she) a Man not Tall nor Squat,

But a good handsom Fellow, (mark ye that ?)
This Youth and you 'tis likely may do well,
If he escape but one—they call her *Nell*.
But if they two should chance to lye together,
He'll break the Heart of you, and of his Father.
Who this *Nell* was, I cou'd not chuse but wonder ;
But now I know who 'tis—a Pox confound her !
I'll make *Cassandra* Liar tho', in part ;
You've vex'd me, but you ne'er shall break my Heart.
This very Whore I speak on, ran away
With such another Fellow t'other Day,
And when her Cloaths were gone, and Mony lavish'd,
She came and told her Husband she was ravis! 'd.
I'm sure I'm true, for here since you were gone
Have been some loving Boobies of the Town,
One of the Fellows surely is a Satyr,
He follows me, and swears he'll watch my Water :
We have a Servant come—pretends to Physick,
He hath a Cure for any one that is sick ;
He cures the Tooth-ach ; if your Finger's cut,
A Plaister to it presently he'll put ;
Freckles i'th' Face he cures, and takes off Pimples,
H'ath taught me too the use of Herbs and Simples :
But I must beg my fellow-Servant's Pardon,
'Gainst Love there is no Herb nor Flow'r i'th Garden :
For this Disease I must rely upon ye,
Come and live here again, you'll cure *Oenone*.

PENELOPE to ULYSSES,

Lately Translated out of

OVID;

Now BURLESQU'D.

The ARGUMENT.

There hapning a Rebellion in Scotland, *in that Army
which went under the Command of the Duke;* Ulysses
*went Voluntier. The Rebels being quell'd, the Army
return'd home; but* Ulysses *lay loitring at some Inn
in the Road; which when his Careful Wife* Penelope
*understood, she sent him this Epistle; giving him an
Account how Affairs stood at home.*

Y Our poor *Penelope* admires that you
  Should ever use a Woman as you do!
Now ev'ry Soldier's at his own Aboad,
You, like a Sot, lye tippling on the Road:

You are not left behind 'em as a Spy,
T'inform, in case of second Mutiny:
The Devil of Hell will have that Fellow surely,
Who first began this plaguy Hurly-burly,
Had it not been for this unlucky Fight,
Y'ad stuck to work all Day :—to me at Night.

  Poor I must drudge at home all sorts of Weather,
And knit,—as Heav'n and Earth would come to-
    gether :
Twirling a Wheel, I sit at home —hum-drum,
And spit away my Nature on my Thumb :
Thus while I spin, you, like a careful Spouse,
Go reeling up and down from House to House.
Being you staid so long, I did conjecture
You had been maul'd by *Sauny*, the *Scotch* Hector :
Old *Nestor's* Son, that Fool, stood just by you,
When's empty Scull, they say, was split in two :
And, when he dropt, for all you are so stout,
You wish'd your self at home, in shitten Clout.
Yet after all, *Ulysses*, I am glad
You are alive, though you're a scurvy Lad.

  Our Neighbours here all Day do tittle tattle,
And talk of nothing else but Blood and Battle;
Were you at home, you could not chuse but Laugh
To hear 'em Crack and Bounce, now they are Safe :
Perhaps when Three or Four of them are met,
And round about a Kitchin-Table set,
There's such a Noise, a Clutter and a Din,

The Rebel *Scots* are routed o'er again.
  Some with Tobacco-Pipes upon a Table,
Do valiantly demonstrate to the Rabble
The Foes chief Strength; with that another Spark
Hamilton's House describes; a third, the Park;
Another spills some Ale upon the Bench,
And, with his Finger, learns you to Entrench;
One acts how fierce our valiant Soldiers ran on,
Dismounts a Can, and tells you 'tis a Cannon;
Another cries, Neighbours, observe and look,
This Pot's Sir *Thomas*, and this Glass the Duke.
Thus while the Husbands draw this bloody Scheme,
The Wives, behind their Chairs, are in a Dream;
Nay, some of 'em (I question whether 'ts true)
Do tell some mighty Deed perform'd by you;
That, being provok'd, you like a valiant **Man** drew,
And cut a *Scotch*-man's Luggs off by St. *Andrew*.
  I'm ne'er the nearer, though they're overcome;
If you'll not mind your Bus'ness here at Home:
For my own part, I would not care a Pin
If they were still in Arms, and you in mine:
Pry'thee, come home; I cannot chuse but wonder
What a God's-name you can be doing yonder.
By ev'ry Post and Carrier to the North
I've sent more Paper than your Neck is worth:
I've sent to *Hull*, to *Berwick*, and to *Grantham*,
I might as well have sent a Post to *Bantam*.
Perhaps some Tapster's Wife subdues your Heart,
9*

Or else her Drink's so strong you cannot part :
And, when you're Drunk, Lord, how your Tongue
    does run,
That you've a House well Furnish'd here in Town,
In which your Wife (or rather, Drudge) doth dwell
As constantly at home, as Snail in Shell.
(But yet, when I remember parting Kisses,
Then, then methinks thou shouldst be true, *Ulysses.)*

    My Father says you're drown'd i'th watry Main ;
The old Man jokes, and bids me Wed again ?
His Counsel, like himself is still unsound,
I'd rather he were hang'd than you were drown'd.

    Every Day here comes a sort of Fellows,
Enow to make a foolish Husband jealous,
From *Whetstone's*-Park, *Moorfields*, or such like Places,
Fellows with Cuts and Trenches in their Faces ;
There are but Seven Fingers amongst Four,
And here they domineer, and swear, and roar :
Two of 'em say, they have been vast Commanders,
The other trail'd a Pike with you in *Flanders ;*
There's one of 'em, they call him, Merry *Robert,*
He, in a merry Way, broke up the Cubboard ;
Here has been *Irus* too, that *Irish* Thief,
Wh'ath eaten up a Surloin of Roast-Beef ;
What signifies my Father or my self,
We can't secure our Meat upon the Shelf ?
What great Defence can Nurse or little Boy make
Against a Fellow with a Horse's Stomach ?

The little Rogue, your Son, was almost drown'd,
Padling about he tumbl'd in the Pond,
But we recover'd him with much ado,
I hope he'll prove a better Man than you.
    In short, if speedily you do not come,
You will be eaten out of House and Home :
The old Man's crazy, we from him must part ;
And I have laid your Usage so to Heart,
That I am grown so wither'd now with Grief,
I look—more like your Mother, than——

                    Your faithful Wife,

                        PENELOPE.

PHÆDRA to HIPPOLYTUS.

The ARGUMENT.

Theseus *having made his Escape out of* France *with* Phædra —*(whose Sister* Ariadne *he deserted at* Calais) *when he came into* England *marry'd her, and brought her home to a Farm-House near* Putney *in* Surrey, *which he Rented of one Mr.* Jove; *which House during his Travel (or rather his Ramble) he committed to his Son* Hippolytus, *who was a great Hunter, a handsome Fellow, and a Woman-hater; for which two last Reasons* Phædra *his Mother, after she had acquainted her self with her Neighbours and Household Affairs, fell desperately in Love; insomuch that nothing would serve her but carnal Copulation with her Son-in-Law; to accomplish which she humbly entreats him by this Letter to consider her Condition.*

TO you, my Lad, I send this am'rous Scroul,
    Wishing you Health, with all my Heart and
        Soul;
Your Mother, and your Lover does beseech,

That with these Lines you wou'd not wipe your
    Breech:
Thank God, my Father gave his Children Breeding,
And taught us all, our Writing and our Reading.
By Letters Men have News, and Women find
Which Way and how their Sweet-hearts are inclin'd.
Thrice I resolv'd to tell you all I thought,
But for my Blood I cou'd not get it out:
I just began to say——My dearest *Poll*,
Then laugh'd, and turn'd aside, and ruin'd all;
Tho' 'tis no laughing matter, for I own
I love the very Ground thou tread'st upon.
I'll tell thee, *Poll*, and mark thee what I say,
If Love thou sullenly dost disobey,
Tho' he's a Boy, not half so big as you,
Yet Fairy-like he'll Pinch you Black and Blew;
On a full Speed your Horse he'll lead astray,
And like a Hare he'll cross you in your Way.
If he Assaults—you cannot beat him off,
Either with hunting Pole or Quarter-Staff.
H'ath sworn, (tho' to your Father I am Wed,)
To bind you fast, and bring you to my Bed.
'Tis true your Strength is great, his only Art,
You pitch the Bar, and he can throw a Dart,
What need I use these Words? dear *Polly*—come,
Let us Embrace, your Father's not at Home.
You know my Reputation's very great,
Who'd guess that you and I shou'd do the Feat.

Oh how I'm stung, I have as little Ease,
As if I had disturb'd a Hive of Bees.
I purr and purr, just like our Tabby Cat,
As if I knew not what I would be at:
When Young, I cou'd have cur'd these am'rous Stings
With Cariots, Radishes, or such like Things;
Now there's no Pleasure in such earthly Cures,
I must have Things apply'd as warm as yours.
Where lies the Blame, art thou not Strong, and Young?
Who wou'd not gather Fruit that is well hung?
Or who can call't a Sin when we have done,
Main't I have leave to hug my Husband's Son?
Suppose our Landlord *Jove*, that gallant Wight,
Had a Months Mind to lodge with me one Night;
Nay——if his Lady too should give Consent,
For you I'd quit him, though he'd quit his Rent.
Since you'll not hunt in this my softer Place,
Where I should get the better of the Chase;
Since the large Fields and Woods you rummage
        through,
Disdaining my poor little Cunny——borough;
I'll follow you o'er Ditches and thro' Boggs,
And whoop and hollow after all the Dogs:
I'll speak to th' Hounds so well, Hey! *Fowler, Bowman,*
That none, but you, shou'd know I am a Woman:
I'll praise your Greyhound *Delia,* when you course,
She shall my Mistress be, and I'll be yours.
... der a Hedge I'll squat down like a Hare,

And you alone shall find me sitting there.
Sometimes upon a Horse I'll get astride,
And after you, as I were mad I'll ride;
For all our Generation have been so,
When they're in Love they know not what they do.
You've heard that Mistress *Europe* was my Grandam;
She went away with *Jupiter* at Random.
Pasiphae, my Mother, was so full
Of strange Vagaries, that she suck'd a Bull.
My Husband with my Sister lay—or rather
I should have told you that it was your Father.
Poor *Adne* was stark Mad for him, and now
I am (God knows) as mad in Love with you:
So that between the Father and the Son,
There are two Sisters like to be undone.
I never shall forget with what a Grace
You drest your self in order for the Chase;
Your Visage not too Red, but only Tann'd,
Of the same Colour with your brawny Hand.
An ancient Bever on your Head you put,
Like a three-Pigeon Pye, in Corners cut.
A little Jacket, made of blewish Green,
Which had the Death of many a Badger seen.
Your Hair your own, which shew'd you not debauch'd,
Not nicely trim'd, for here and there 'twas notch'd.
I hate your Fellows with their powder'd Wiggs,
As m'Husband us'd to say, they look like Prigs.
You'd lasting Breeches made of Buckskin Leath

To keep the fundamental Parts from Weather.
But when you reach'd your Hanger from the Bed,
Another Weapon came into my Head.
Not all your Days can give you such Delight,
As half the Sport I'll shew you in a Night,
Delia's your Joy, *Delia* does you bewitch;
Can you neglect a Christian, for a Bitch?
Cephalus, your Companion and old Crony,
Valu'd a Dog better than ready Mony.
He'd get upon a Horse, though half asleep,
Ready to Hunt before the Day did peep;
But when h'ad once tasted *Aurora*'s Sweets,
He found out better Game between the Sheets;
For then, unless she pleas'd, he durst not say,
(Nor did he wish) that it wou'd e'er be Day.
Why should not we consent to try our Skill?
I'm certain you and I can do as well.
Therefore dear *Poll*, I offer very fair,
Under *Barn-Elmes* I'll met [meet] you if you dare;
Since none but Country Sports can humour you,
I'll Wrastle with you there a Fall or two;
Though o' my Conscience I believe you'll throw me,
But if you shou'd, perhaps it won't undo me;
And when you have me down among the Trees,
You wonton Rogue, you may do what you please.
We'd no such Opportunity before;
Your Father is at *London* with his Whore.
Therefore I think 'tis but a just Design,

To Cuckold him, and pay him in his Coin.
Besides he ne'er was marry'd to your Mother,
He first whor'd her, and then he took another.
What Kindness or Respect ought we to have
For such a Villain and perfidious Knave?
This should not trouble, but provoke us rather
With all the Speed we can to lye together.
I am no Kin to you, nor you to me,
They call it Incest but to terrifie.
Lovers Embraces are Lascivious Tricks,
'Mongst musty Puritants and Schismaticks.
Did not our Master *Jove* chuse him a Mistress,
Who should it be but one of his own Sisters?
There's no engendring can be truly good,
But when we fancy that we're of a Blood.
Under the Names of Mother and of Son,
What pretty pleasant Actions may be done?
All they will say, because I'm kind to Thee,
I'm Mother both in Law and Equity.:
Take Heart of Grace, be not afraid of Spyes,
I care not if there were ten Thousand Eyes;
I'll leave the Door without the Bolt or Lock:
What if they saw us in our Shirt or Smock.
Nay I'll suppose we should be seen in Bed,
What can there to our Prejudice be said?
That you came wet and dripping from the Chace,
And I'd a Mind to give you my warm Place.
I did not think to've said so much in haste,

But Love like Murder must come out at last :
The Fort lyes open, therefore scorn it not,
But come with Speed, and enter on the Spot.
Let us imagine now the worst can happen,
Suppose that you and I were taken napping ;
And *Theseus* says, Be gone you filthy Whore ;
Away you Rogue, and so he shuts the Door.
What if does, why then for *France* with Speed,
We shall be there supply'd with all we need.
My Father dwells at *Paris* in good Credit,
And well to pass is he, though I have said it ;
There he's as well known as Begger knows his Dish,
We'll live as bravely then as Heart can wish :
Therefore make haste, Dream not of any Harms,
Thou'lt be secure enough within my Arms.
When you go out, may you be sure of Game ;
May your Horse never tire, nor happen lame :
At a Default may the Dogs never be,
May *Delia* bring forth Whelps as good as she.
May you i'th' Field ne'er want a Draught of Beer,
Or Bread and Cheese, or such like hunting Cheer ;
While I sit pining for you here at home,
When I have cry'd out both my Eyes you'll come.

HYPSIPYLE to *JASON.*

Lately Translated out of

OVID;

Now BURLESQU'D.

The ARGUMENT.

Jason, *a* quondam *Foot-man, with some others, the nimblest of the same Function, joined their Stocks, and purchas'd a Silver-Bowl, which they ran for from* Barnet *to St.* Albans; *but before the Day of the Match, one* Medæa, *a Gipsey, and Strouler in those Parts, took a more than ordinary Fancy towards* Jason, *whom she so dieted with new-laid Eggs, or what the Devil it was else (she being suspected of Witchcraft,) that he won the Plate; and beat two famous Foot Jockeys,* Whipping-Tom *and* Teague : Hypsipyle, *his Wife, whom he had deserted, hearing of his good Success, and withal, of his Love-Intrigue with* Medæa, *caused this Epistle to be sent to him.*

From So-hoe *Fields*, Feb. 27. 16⁷⁹⁄₈₀.

Husband,

THE Neighbours in our Alley do relate
    That at St. *Albans* you have won the Plate :
How easie a Matter had it been for you,
T'have sent poor *Hyp.* your Wife, a *George* or two ?
    Did I, when *Flannel* was both dear and scarce,
Make you Trunk-hose to your ungrateful Arse ?
I sew'd so long, my Fingers still do ake,
And, in all Conscience, I deserve my Snack.
    I can hear something, though I keep at home ;
I hear, y'have beaten *Teague* and *Whipping Tom :*
You ran so swift and strong, the People say,
You bore down all that stood but in your Way :
Before your founder'd Fellows could come up
You won the Match, aud seis'd the *Caudla-Cup.*
I know, y'have been a Rogue, and done me Wrong ;
Yet I'd hear this from your own flatt'ring Tongue.
But why should'st thou e'er hope for that, poor *Hypsi*,
Since *Jason* loves a Bacon-visaged Gipsey.
As I was washing, th'other Day at Door,
There came a Scoundril, ill-look'd Son-of-a-Whore,
Who, jeering, ask'd if I were Madam *Jason ?*
I'd like t'have thrown Soap-suds his ugly Face on.

Said I, I'm *Jason*'s Wife for want of better;
Have you brought Mony from him, or a Letter?
How does he do? is he not very fine?
Come, come, let's see, I'm sure h'ath sent me Coin.
Quoth he, By God of Heav'n, not a Souze;
He only bid me see you at your House.
The Fellow told m'a Tale of Cock and Bull;
At last, I ask'd about your Tawny Trull.
He said, *Medæa*'s your beloved Gipsey,
And that you're often seen together tipsey;
But, he believ'd 'twas but a Trick of Youth:
A Trick; said I, the Devil stop your Mouth.
   Would I'd been lash'd and whipt the City round
That Day I marry'd thee, loose Vagabond:
The Hangman in Disguise read Common-pray'r
When we were match'd, a very Hopeful Pair:
Curst be the Time I did admit you first,
And strove to quench your everlasting Thirst:
What Plague possest me when I brought you home?
This was no Place to run with *Whipping-Tom.*
   If I had taken but my Sisters Counsel,
Y'had never set your flat-Foot o'er the Groundsel:
She bid me exercise the Fork and Spit;
We'd then good Goods, but now the De'il a bit.
   'Twas well enough a Year, nay, almost Two;
What Fury hath Possession of you now?
Villain, remember when you went away,
How oft you Damn'd your self, you would not stay;
11

And smoothly said, No Place shall us divide ;
A Curse upon your base dissembling Hide :
I was so Big that I could hardly Tumble,
Yet I believ'd your Oaths, and durst not grumble :
Said you, Dear *Hypsi*, know that I am Dead,
If I don't come before you're brought to Bed ;
You look'd like Air, with Breeches close to Thighs,
I fancy'd you'd be back within a trice :
When you were gone I to the Garret crept,
To see how nimbly o'er the Fields you tript ;
As swift you went, so swift Return you'ld make,
But all this Haste was for that Bitch's sake :
Why do I rub my Windows, wash my Room,
Expecting still your Rogueship would come home ?
    'Twould never vex me, if you were not seen
With such a damn'd confounded nasty Quean :
A Witch, a Bitch, in whom the Devil dwells,
Whose Face is made of Grease and Wallnut-shells.
Master, quoth she, e'er from this Town you stir
You'll lose, (that is your Pockets pick'd by her.)
A plaguy Jade, who curses Night and Noon,
And houls, and heaves her Arse against the Moon,
Contemning her as Authress of the Flow'rs ;
Railing at all our Sex, and Poxing yours :
No Childing Woman doth in Travel linger,
But tow'rds her Pain the Fiend holds up a Finger :
She'll ride a Stick ; when Sow is brought to Bed,
The Pigs have no more Life than Pigs of Lead :

She, with the Mother, at a Door will wheedle,
And, in her Infant's Heart, will stick a Needle :
This I believe, what e'er of me you think,
Sh'ath put some Rotten-post into your Drink.

'Tis strange, that I should suffer all these Wrongs
From her, whom I would scorn to touch with Tongs.
You'll lose the Name of beating *Tom* and *Teague*,
Whilst with this Whore you do continue League :
Nay, some do very confidently say't,
'Twas by her Witch-craft that you won the Plate :
Some think her Devil, others, new-laid Eggs,
Made you so fast advance your Bandy-leggs :
What can you find in such a Punk as she,
Who from a Dunghil brings her Pedigree ?
My Father dwells at Sign of *Golden-Can*,
An honest Vict'ler, a substantial Man :
'Tis true, they say, he is a drunken Sot ;
What then ; i'th' Parish he pays Scot and Lot :
Old *Bacchus*, the Wine-cooper, was my Grandsire ;
Let her produce such Kindred, if she can, Sir :
Her Children have been gotten in a Bog,
By some large pintled Wolf, or Mastive Dog :
My Babes were neither got nor whelp'd i'th' Streets,
I labour'd for them 'twixt a Pair of Sheets :
That they are yours, I'm sure you need not doubt,
For they're as like as if y'had spit them out :
Could they have gone, alone I'd made 'em amble
To your Apartment underneath a Bramble ;
11*

But I consider'd how your Whore would treat 'em,
Nay, it is ten to one, the Hag would eat 'em;
Or else, perhaps, she'd stick their tender Skins
All full of Sparables, or crooked Pins;
Since of her own sh'ath Murther'd many a Brat,
Would she spare mine; oh! never tell me that.
Methinks I see you and the Hell-born Toad
Engendring in a Tree that's near the Road:
Suppose you were pursu'd, as you're a Thief;
Where would you fly? where would you find Relief?
What if your self and yonder Devil's Dam
Should come to me, and try if you could sham?
Sure I should make you very welcome both,
And entertain you nobly by my Troth.

I should towards you make some relenting Heart,
But 'tis my Goodness more than your Desert:
And, for your Fire-brand there, that loathsome Hag,
I would contrive the greatest Pain and Plague:
Her Nose being slit, to make her look more Grim,
Like a *Spread-Eagle* on her Face should seem:
Her coarse black Skin should from her Flesh be rent;
I'd run a Spit into her Fundament:
And, *Jason*, this thy Punishment should be,
Thou should'st eat those, so oft have swallow'd thee.

But since it must not be, I am contented
To let my Spleen in cursing her be vented:
May she all Sustenance for ever lack,
Until she takes her Child from off her Back,

And puts it in her Belly for a Nuncheon,
And for the Fact be thrown into a Dungeon:
May she be burnt to Cinders as a Witch,
And you be hang'd for loving of a Bitch.

Yours, as you have us'd her

HYPSIPYLE.

For John Jason, *to be left at his Apartment, in a hollow Tree, between* Barnet *and St.* Albans.

PARIS to HELEN.

The ARGUMENT.

Paris *had liv'd a great while in Obscurity, at last being own'd by Alderman* Priam *a Rich Old Citizen, and receiv'd as his Son, he set up for a Gentleman; but very well knowing he could not be rightly accomplish'd without a Mistress, and hearing Fame speak* viva voce *in the praise of one* Helen, *who liv'd somewhere in the* North; *he was at her House receiv'd, and during the absence of* Menelaus *her Husband, he endeavour'd to break his Mind to her; but being not thorough-pac'd in Gentility, his Modesty got the upper Hand of his Inclination, therefore he presently had recourse to his Pen, and writes her this conceited Letter.*

Reely and from my Heart, without compelling,
    I wish all Health and Happiness to *Helen:*
For if you're Sick, I'm sure to suffer Pain;
As I'm a Lover and a Gentleman.

I need not tell you that I'm off o'th' Hooks,
Your Ladiship discerns it by my Looks :
For you, whose Eyes have such a piercing quickness,
May see I'm overgrown with the Green-sickness :
So that upon the whole and perfect Matter,
I am your Servant, but I seem your Daughter.
I could eat Wall as well as white Bread Crum,
But fear to eat you out of House and home.
For this Distemper I've read many Cures,
But the sole Power of healing must be Yours :
Your Holiness (I cannot call you less,
That doth on Earth perform such Miracles)
Your Holiness, I say, within few Weeks,
May fetch a lively Colour in my Cheeks.
But if we are too long e're we begin,
I'm apt to fear it may corrupt within.
'Tis Love, 'tis Love, that makes me Toss and **Tumble**,
And in my Entrails does like Jollup rumble :
'Tis as impossible you should not see't,
As 'tis to hid the Pox both small **and great**.
'Tis Love, you know th' Effects of that Disease,
Therefore pray fall to Work when e'er you please.
If at these Lines you do not jeer nor jybe,
There is some Hopes you may receive the Scribe.
And, Madam, know, I did engage the Stars,
Before I durst engage in *Cupid's* Wars.
This is a grand Affair, I had been silly
T'ave ventur'd on't without consulting *Lilly ;*

To him I went for my own happy Ends,
And all the Planets he hath made my Friends,
And above all, the most pellucide *Venus*,
Hath promis'd there should be a Job between us:
She knoweth best what's good for you and me,
She does command our Fates and Pow'rs, d'ye see.
Without her leave no living Lover stirs ;
Paris, said she, put on your Boots and Spurs.
She did consent I should ascend my Horse,
And toward your Mansion bend my glorious Course.
Never by her was Riding yet forbidden,
Her Goddess-ship with Pleasure has been ridden.
My Heart's upon the racking trot—alas!
But she can bring it to a gentle Pace.
Next, Madam, know, your Sight was no Surprize,
I lov'd you by my Ears as well as Eyes.
Your Fame hath much out-sounded the Report
Of the great Guns, at taking of a Fort.
I came not here to seek terrestial Pelf,
I made this Progress for your heav'nly self.
The Womb o'th' Universe if I should rifle,
To your more secret Parts 'twere but a Trifle.
To see your ancient Pile I do not range,
We have more lofty Fabricks near th' Exchange.
'Twas for you sake I spurr'd my stubborn Steed,
For you alone thro' thick and thin I rid.
You're mine, what desp'rate Mortal dares gainsay't ?
Sure I may take my Planet's Word for that.

I 2

I fain would tell your Ladiship a Dream,
If it would not too great a Trouble seem,
My Mother dreamt, when she with me was quick,
She should bring forth a lighted Fagot-stick:
I am that Fagot-stick, I burn a pace,
Oh quench me, Madam, in your watring—place.
I've taken fire at you, as a Match at Tinder:
Cool me, or else your Servant is a Cinder.
This was my Mother's Dream, I now design,
Under Correction, to tell you mine.

　I laid me down to sleep one Summers Day,
Under the Shade of a new Stack of Hay;
For we poor Lovers, such is our hard case,
Are glad to take a Nap in any Place;
Three naked Ladies came, I well remember,
As naked as the Trees are—in *December;*
They told me they'd be judg'd alone by me,
Which was the most deserving of the Three;
The first would bribe me with a Purse of Gold;
My Judgment's neither to be bought nor sold:
The second offer'd me a tilting Sword,
Knowing I ne'er would take an angry Word:
But says the Third, and in my Face she giggled,
With such poor Toyes you're not to be inveigled,
But if you value me above the rest,
Then know, young Man, you are for ever blest.
Within a little time you shall arrive,
Where a resplendent Country Dame does live;

First you must Court her like an humble Beggar,
At last she'll yield, and you may lay your Leg—o'er ;
The Prize is yours, said I, you ought to take't,
I kiss'd her lower Parts, and so I wak'd.
My Dream is out, for thus I do explain it,
You are the Country Dame, and she the Planet.
Without Delay I put on my Accoutring,
And with full Speed, I came to you a Suit'ring.
But just as I was putting Foot in Stirrup,
Drinking with Friends a parting Cup of Syrrup,
My Sister came to th'Door, a mad young Lass,
Her Name's *Cassandra,* but we call her *Cass;*
Brother, quoth she, beware, beware, I say,
You do not meet a Fireship by the Way:
A strange wild Wench, I hope she did not mean
That any where your Ladiship's unclean ;
Heav'ns forbid : Good Soul, she meant no more
Than Flames of Love, as I have said before.
Being arriv'd at this your decent House,
Whom should I meet but your Illustrious Spouse?
He brought a Tankard out of good March Beer,
Cold Pork and Butter, and such houshold Cheer ;
He ask'd—if ever I Tobacco took,
I said I'd take a Pipe—but cou'd not Smoak ;
He shew'd m'his Garden, and his fine young Trees,
His Barn, his Stable, and his House of Ease :
I said 'twas wondrous pretty—but my Mind
Still ran on what my Planet had design'd.
12*

At last you came with such a dazling Grace,
I thought the Sun and Moon was in your Face,
Lillies and Roses, Pinks and Violets,
Your Looks were loaded with the vernal Sweets ;
Your poor Adorer was in such Amaze,
I vow and swear I knew not where I was ;
Before I spoke I fell to private Pray'r ;
" Planet, I thank thee for thy tender Care ;
" Now thou hast rais'd my Bliss to such a Pitch,
" I humbly beg, that thou'dst go thorough stitch.
At last I spake, and bow'd in seemly wise,
And paid Obeysance to your sparkling Eyes ;
Your Beauty's greater than your Fame did boast,
So is a May-Pole taller than a Post.
I've heard, you once conferr'd your gracious Favour
On *Theseus*, who was thought a cunning Shaver ;
With him your Ladiship has play'd some Gambols,
Frolicks y'have had, and many pleasant Rambles.
But, by your Leave, your Lover was a Clown,
For leaving your bright Eminence so soon ;
D'ye think that *Paris* would have served you so,
Would he have let Illustrious *Helen* go ?
By *Stix* and *Acheron* your Servant swears,
Rather than part with you, he'll lose his Ears ;
When that Hour comes for which we both were born,
And soon 'twill come, or Planet is forsworn ;
When we shall lye entranc'd—entranc'd I say,
Then if you have the Heart to go, you may ;

Hasten, forsooth, hasten the happy Job,
For 'till't be done——my Heart will shout and throb :
'Tis very fit that you and I should join,
Your Family's very good, and so is mine.
My Father fin'd for Alderman, long since,
He's now grown Rich, and lives like any Prince.
If you wou'd once make *London* your Aboad,
You'd hate a Village as you'd hate a Toad.
Oh how your Ladiship wou'd stare to see
Our City Dames in all their Bravery.
They've Petticoats with Lace above their Knees
Of Gold and Silver, or of Point *Venice ;*
Cornets and lofty Tow'rs upon the Head,
And wond'rous Shapes of which you never read.
How ill a Pinner with a narrow Lace,
Becomes the Beauty of so bright a Face ?
A fairer Face no Mortal e're laid Lips to,
And I believe there are not whiter Hips too.
Too white too [to] mingle with a Husband's Thighs ;
When I but think of that, my Flesh does rise.
When towards me sometimes a Glance does pass,
Your poor Adorer looketh like an Ass.
For if I should return you Look for Look,
I fear your Husband will begin to smoak ;
And I'll be hang'd, if ever *Menelaus,*
By any am'rous Look of mine, betray us ;
Were it not at your Table, I'd abuse him,
For thrusting his great Paw into your Bosom :

That Watry Fist between your Breasts does seem
Like a brown *George* dropt in a Bowl of Cream.
I'm mad to see him draw his Chair so close,
And kiss, and hugg you, underneath my Nose.
Then I go out, pretending to make Water,
Seeming to take no notice of the matter :
To all true Hearts I drink a Cup of Wine,
A Health that does imply both yours and mine ;
Then seeming Drunk, I tell some strange Romance,
And lay the Scene in *Italy* or *France* ;
Of some bright Lady, and her brisk—Gall—ant ;
By which two Lovers, you and I are meant.
But, Madam, to write more of this were Nonsense,
My Planet has contriv'd the Bus'ness long-since ;
By curious Search I something can discover,
'Tis in your Blood—you're born to be a Lover.
What think you Lady, of your Father *Jove* ?
Shew me a Town-bull has been more in Love.
Your Mother *Leda* too, who gave you suck,
Has she not been as good as ever struck ?
When sh'ad a lusty Youth between her Thighs,
What d'ye think ? would *Leda* cry to rise ?
Your Parents being as right as ever pist,
If you should be precise, you wou'd be hist.
But if you must be constant to one Man,
With me to *London* make what haste you can.
There we'll provide a little Winter House,
And you shall pass for my renowned Spouse.

By what I see your Husband does approve,
That in his Absence here I should make Love.
Or wou'd he else have gone,——under pretence
To buy a Horse—a hundred Miles from hence ?
The Bus'ness seems to me, as plain a Case,
As is the Noise [nose] upon your beauteous **Face.**
To let you know that I should be no Clog,
Did he not say, Love me and love my Dog ?
Nelly, said he, be kind unto my Guest,
And let his Entertainment be the *Best.*
I presently his Meaning understood,
If yours be not the *Best*—then nothing's good.
You see your Husband orders our **Affairs,**
Therefore, dear Madam, do not hang an Arse,
But let's away to *London—Crop* does wait,
Saddled and Bridled at the Garden-gate ;
Crop's a good natur'd Beast—and carries double,
And will not think your Ladiship a trouble.
Strike while the Iron's hot, my Love is fervent,
Get up, and ride behind——

Your humble Servant

Paris.

HELEN's Answer to PARIS.

The ARGUMENT.

Helen *having receiv'd his Letter, at first seems wonder-*
fully displeas'd at his Impudence, in attempting a
Lady of her unspotted Fame ; who was bred and born
in the Town where she liv'd, and was never call'd
Whore. At length the Storm's over, and she Tacks
about, giving him an Assurance of her readiness to
comply, but doubts her Gallant wo'not be constant. In
plain English She's as willing as he.

Your Letter's wrot in such a filthy Stile,
    I did not think an Answer worth my while,
'Till I consider'd you might offer Vi'lence,
And take Advantage of a Woman's Silence.
    13

I'm sure you have not wanted Drink or Food;
I wonder in my Heart you'll be so rude.
'Tis fine y'faith—because you come from *London*,
You think a Country Body must be run down.
You of your Entertainment here may brag,
You were not us'd as if you had the Plague.
My Husband did receive you as a *Friend*,
And would you to his Wife now prove a *Fiend?*
Perhaps you'll say of me, when you are gone,
Helen! a Lady!—*Helen's* but a Clown.
I'll own the Name, since you can say no more,
I'd rather be a Clown, then call'd a Whore :
Yet for all that, though I keep Cows and Daries,
I can behave my self as well as *Paris :*
Tho' I don't fleer like a young wanton Girle,
Yet you shall seldom see me Frown or Snarle.
Tho' you such Breeding and such Manners own,
Let me deal plainly w'ye—I think you've none.
Or could you else believe me so untrue,
To leave my Spouse, and run away with you?
Because a Fellow once did pick me up,
You think I'm to be stoln by ev'ry Fop.
He knew not whether I was Man or Woman,
But you conclude from thence that I am common.
When he perceiv'd *that I was none of those,*
He very fairly brought me to my House.
And since I'm gotten quit of Master *Theseus,*
Our *Paris* wou'd be nibbling too, God bless us!—

Though by my Troth I cannot blame your Love,
If I were sure that you wou'd constant prove.
D'ye think I should not be in dainty pickle,
If I should run away with one that's fickle?
You urg'd to me th'Example of my Mother,
As if the Daughter shou'd be such another.
You don't consider *Læda* was betray'd,
By one that courted her in Masquerade.
She thought sh'ad met a harmless Plume of Feather,
But at *long-run* he prov'd a Stallion rather.
His Family's the best in all the County,
All that you live by's but a Tradesman's Bounty.
But that's all one, where-ever Love prevails,
Mony's no more than pairing [paring] of my Nails.
Sometimes I think you Love me when you look
With Eyes unmov'd, just like a Pig that's stuck;
And dabble with your Fingers in my Palm,
And use to call the Moisture of it,—Balm.
If in the Glass I leave a little Drop,
You'd say I'll drink your Suffs—and suck it up.
Helen you carv'd with Penknife on the Gate,
And I wrote *Paris* just a top of that.
These are shrew'd signs of Love, and without doubt
You'd give a Leg or Arm to have a Bout.
Tho' you are not the first Man by a hundred,
That has seen me, and lov'd and gaz'd and wondred.
If you at first had come into our Town,
And courted *Helen* in a Grogram Gown,
13*

When I was but a silly Soul, God knows,
You might have made a Bridge of *Menel's* Nose.
Now he commands in chief your Suit is van [vain],
To all true Lovers Marriage is a Bane.
But why should *Paris* for a Mistress long,
Since in your Sleep your Fancy is so strong?
You can see three stark Naked at a time,
And take your Choice of Beauties in a Dream :
Yet you left Honour, Wealth, and God knows what,
And all for me—a pretty Fancy that.
I know 'tis Wheedle,——but if all were true,
It is no more than I would do for you.
You guess my want of Skill, by being so plain,
For I'm not us'd to write to any Man,
Except t' a Millener, (my Husband's Cozen)
Who sends me Gloves, and Ribbands by the dozen,
Well——since it must be so——let's be discreet,
Let not our Town take Notice that we meet :
For they suspect already you're a Wencher,
There is not such a Place on Earth for Censure.
Yet I can't see, why we should be so nice,
I like you—by my Husband's own Advice.
I cou'd not chuse but laugh to hear him say,
Pray Love your Guest when I am gone away :
And all the while that *Menelaus* tarries.
You are committed to the Charge of *Paris.*
The Charge ! Let us examine well the Word,
Whether he meant your Charge at Bed and Board ;

Why should he not mean both as well as one?
He knows—how much I hate to lye alone.
In my weak Judgment, 'tis an easie Case,
You are in all Things to supply his Place.
But for the Master-ship you're like to tug,
Before you have me at the closest Hug.
'Twill seem to me, if you some Force do use,
As if I had a Maidenhead to lose.
Lord! how I write; if I were to be damn'd,
I cou'd nor [not] say't—I should be so asham'd.
If I consent, I'll hold you any Mony,
You'll serve me as you did your dear *Oenone :*
She hop'd she shou'd be wedded in the Church,
Instead of that you left her in the Lurch.
But if we now were toward *London* jogging,
'Tis ten to one some Puppy would be dogging,
Or else some Neighbour on the Road wou'd stay us,
And ask me after Mr. *Menelaus.*
Or we shall hear the Country People say,
Would you believe that she should run away?
Marry not handsome Wives by this Example,
Since pretty Mistress *Helen*'s on the Ramble.
I'm strangely affraid of seeing Mr. *Priam,*
How shall I tremble when he asks who I—am.
Though for my Life I shall not hold from Laughter,
If *Hecuba* should say, Your Servant, Daughter.
But above All 'tis *Hector* that I dread,
That *Hector* certainly will break my Head.

Who'd think you two from the same Mother came,
He's like a Lyon, you are like a Lamb.
Let *Hector* prosper with his senseless Huffing,
'Tis *knowing nothing now* that makes a Ruffian.
While *Paris* shall be skill'd in Lovers Arts,
And dive into our Sexes Secret Parts;
Now you begin to think 'tis ten to one,
Your Suit is granted, and the Bus'ness done.
But not so fast,——consult my Friend *Clymene*,
No doubt—you'll make the Bus'ness up between ye.
I'm loath to say't my self, she knows my Mind,
And she can tell you how I am inclin'd.
When she informs you what must [be] transacted,
With too much Joy, I fear, you'll run distracted.

F I N I S.

www.ingramcontent.com/pod-product-compliance
Lightning Source LLC
Chambersburg PA
CBHW030541270326
41927CB00008B/1470